Dialectical Behavior Therapy

A Comprehensive Guide to DBT and Using Behavioral Therapy to Manage Borderline Personality Disorder

Table of Contents

Introduction 1

Chapter One: What is DBT? 2

Chapter Two: Core Mindfulness 22

Chapter Three: Distress Tolerance 48

Chapter Four: Interpersonal Effectiveness Skills 78

Chapter Five: Emotion Regulation Skills 114

Chapter Six: DBT and Mental Illnesses 131

Conclusion 162

Resources 163

Introduction

Thank you for taking the time to read this book on Dialectical Behavior Therapy.

This book covers the topic of Dialectical Behavior Therapy, or DBT. In the following chapters, you will learn all about the history of DBT, the four modules that it teaches, and the large number of disorders that it can be used to treat, including borderline personality disorder.

You will soon discover the different applications of DBT and gain an understanding of not only how it is implemented, but also, why it works.

It is my hope that through this book, you will gain a better understanding of human emotions, and the mental health disorders that are becoming increasingly prevalent in modern society.

If after reading this book you decide that DBT is something you would like to pursue, then I strongly encourage you to speak to a therapist or medical professional about beginning treatment. As you will soon find out, Dialectical Behavior Therapy can be truly life changing.

Once again, thanks for choosing this book. I hope you find it to be helpful!

Chapter One: What is DBT?

DBT is short for Dialectical Behavior Therapy. This form of therapy is most effective when implemented alongside cognitive behavioral therapy or CBT; however, the two are very different. The goal of DBT is to replace negative thinking patterns and behaviors with positive thinking patterns and behaviors. DBT is primarily used for people with eating disorders and helps them learn to regulate their emotions, build self-management skills, reduce anxiety and stress, live in the moment, improve personal relationships, and control destructive eating habits.

In addition to eating disorders such as bulimia and anorexia, DBT is also used in the treatment of other mental illnesses such as anxiety, borderline personality disorder, and substance abuse (addictions). It helps patients that have self-destructive habits. It can also help treat people with post-traumatic stress disorder, or people that show severe signs of depression and want to harm themselves or others.

When an individual is undergoing DBT, they will typically partake in three therapeutic settings:

- A classroom where the individual is taking tests, completing assignments, and role-playing ways to interact with other people.

- One-on-one professional therapy where the skills learned are confined and tailored around the individual's personal needs.

- One-on-one phone coaching where the individual can contact their therapist through the phone to receive guidance on how to act or what to do at the moment.

Professional therapists who work with their clients one-on-one will often consult with their patients on a regular basis to keep them motivated and help them navigate through the complicated and complex issues they may be experiencing.

History

In the late 1980s, Dr. Marsha Linehan, a professor and researcher at the University of Washington, and her colleagues developed DBT when they discovered cognitive behavioral therapy did not work successfully in patients who suffered from Borderline Personality Disorder (BPD). Dr. Linehan and her colleagues added strategies to CBT and developed a treatment which addresses the individual needs of those who suffered from BPD.

DBT originates from a philosophical process called "dialectics." Dialectics is the art of explaining or examining the truth of opinions. In this case, with DBT, the "D" is based on the concept that everything has an opposite, and that change only occurs when the opposing force is stronger than the current prevailing force.

Dialectics in DBT -

- Recognizes that change is the only constant and is a process.
- Recognizes that everything is made of opposing forces.
- Combines the most important parts of the opposing factors to form a new meaning, perspective, or outcome in a particular circumstance.
- Holds the Core Dialectic of: Acceptance and Change

Together, the DBT therapist and the client work to resolve contradictions between self-acceptance and change. The aim is to successfully create positive changes in the patient.

A different technique that Linehan and her colleagues created was validation. With validation, alongside the push for positive change, their patients were more likely to cooperate while showing a significant decrease in distress symptoms over the idea of change. With this approach, the therapist reflects the patients' thoughts and actions, making them feel as though what they have done or said "makes sense." This makes the patient feel secure, while the therapist isn't necessarily agreeing that the decisions made by the patient are the best approach to solving their issues.

Linehan and her colleagues created DBT for the purpose of helping people struggling with suicidal tendencies. Since it revolves around regulating your emotions and understanding your intrusive thoughts, DBT was generated under the study of cognitive behavioral therapy but is a subset of the more general classification of CBT. Therapies that exist under the CBT umbrella are: rational emotive behavior therapy, cognitive therapy, rational behavior therapy, rational living therapy, and schema-focused therapy.

However, DBT combines some of these therapies, including the standard techniques from CBT for regulating emotions, mindfulness awareness, and distress tolerance. Some of the exercises in DBT were even derived from Eastern meditative practices. DBT has been proven to be an effective, natural treatment for binge eating, depression, anxiety, and mood disorders such as major depressive disorder, bipolar, substance-induced mood disorders, disruptive mood dysregulation disorder, and borderline personality disorder, to name a few.

The Four Modules

At its simplest, DBT is "the existence of opposites." People will learn the two opposite strategies of acceptance and change. They learn that their experiences and behaviors are valid and that they have to make positive changes to regulate their emotions in order to move forward through difficulties.

DBT is divided into four stages, which are defined by how serious an individual's behaviors are:

- **Stage one** consists of the individual being miserable with "out-of-control" behavior. The goal here is to get the person to become more in control of themselves, their emotions, and their behaviors.

- **Stage two** consists of the individual feeling as if they are living a life of quiet desperation. Although their life-threatening behavior is manageable, they are still suffering. The goal here is to come out of the quiet desperation and into a life full of emotional experiences.

- **Stage three** consists of individual learning to define their personal goals, build self-respect, and discover peace and fulfillment. The goal here is to have the person live a healthy life that balances unhappiness and happiness.

- **Stage four** has the goal of helping the person find a deeper meaning of life through their spiritual existence.

Whether an individual takes on therapy in a group classroom setting, one-on-one in an office setting, or over the phone in the comfort of their own home, they have to implement four modules of DBT.

The four modules – core mindfulness, distress tolerance, interpersonal effectiveness skills, and emotion regulation – are designed to assist individuals in their specific needs for recovery. The intent of these four modules is to help people address their emotions such as depression, anxiety, irritability, or anger. Also, to help them with managing themselves in situations with other relationships (especially chaotic ones), acting on impulse, and dealing with stressful environments, or feelings of emptiness are what the last module works on.

Core mindfulness focuses solely on how to center yourself and focus on the present moment by paying complete attention to everything being done. Distress tolerance helps the client learn acceptance of their current situation, and they learn crisis survival skills to reduce the chances of engaging in problematic behavior. Emotion regulation skills teach the individual how to label emotions, identify problems surrounding the emotions, reduce habits based on their feelings, and increase positive emotions by changing the way they think. Finally, interpersonal effectiveness skills teach useful strategies to ask and go after what they need and want, saying no and not feeling guilty, and coping with close, bonding relationships like friends and family, or intimacy.

Core Mindfulness

Mindfulness skills are commonly taught in Eastern spiritual traditions, and the practice is a key component of DBT. Mindfulness teaches an individual to focus on what is happening in the present. Through mindfulness, individuals learn grounding techniques that help them stay focused on the present moment. If the person becomes anxious or gets stuck in a cycle of overthinking, they can use the techniques they have learned to slow down their mind and focus on what they are doing in that moment rather than on excessively worrying about the past or future.

Distress Tolerance

When emotions run high, it can become difficult to process your feelings. Distress tolerance teaches people how to self-soothe in healthy ways when they feel overwhelmed by emotions. It teaches acceptance and how to calm your thoughts and feelings when dealing with them, rather than avoiding them or becoming overwhelmed by them.

Rather than falling into destructive patterns and acting on impulse, the individual will learn how to make wise decisions about how to act when they feel these intense emotions. Crisis survival skills are taught for the purpose of the individual learning how not to engage in problematic behaviors which can make the situation worse. Problematic behaviors can include blaming or belittling others, refusing to follow rules, throwing temper tantrums in public, using substances such as drugs or alcohol, refusing to eat, or physically and verbally lashing out at others.

Distress tolerance skills also include acceptance skills which are necessary for understanding and accepting your reality, instead of using behaviors to try to change reality or to avoid acknowledging that reality exists.

Interpersonal Effectiveness Skills

Interpersonal effectiveness consists of helping the individual work on their personal relationships. At the same time, interpersonal effectiveness skills help the individual understand their own needs and develop ways to get what they need and to ask for help in healthy ways. This component of DBT involves learning how to respect yourself and others, mastering effective communication, dealing with challenging people, repairing broken relationships, and learning to say no.

Emotion Regulation Skills

These skills allow individuals to understand their own emotions and the core of where these emotions are coming from. It's the art of learning how to deal with overwhelming feelings and how to decrease the intensity of these emotions. The individual will learn about their emotions, why they happen, and how to best approach them when they become too intense.

These four modules are beneficial for helping people that suffer from mood disorders, substance abuse, and eating abnormalities. Group therapy classes usually will meet once per week for two hours, and it takes about twenty-four hours to learn every module in full. In short, it takes approximately twelve weeks of twelve classes to learn every module. People who meet with a therapist or talk to a DBT professional alone usually see someone once a week or bi-weekly for one hour at a time. Classes are best suited for people that are in the third and fourth stage of DBT, whereas people in the first or second stage of DBT will usually benefit more from seeing someone one-on-one.

What is CBT?

Cognitive behavioral therapy is a type of treatment proven to be effective for problems such as depression, anxiety disorders, drug and alcohol issues, marital and relationship problems, eating disorders, and other types of mental illness. CBT is a form of treatment that focuses on how an individual's beliefs, thoughts, and attitudes affect their emotions and behaviors. CBT is used effectively to treat a wide variety of conditions.

Cognitive behavioral therapy is particularly suitable for people who exhibit the following signs and symptoms:

- People who have developed unhelpful thinking patterns, which lead to mental disorders such as anxiety.

- People who often act on emotional impulses, such as anger, which can lead to other psychological problems.

- People who are already suffering from a mental illness or disorder and haven't yet learned sufficient coping skills.

For example, if someone is depressed, their perceptions and interpretations of the world and events around them become distorted. With this distorted take on the world, a person will be more susceptible to maintaining a negative mindset, making harsh accusations, catastrophizing about everything, making mountains out of molehills, or seeing everything in black and white or as good and bad (known as all-or-nothing thinking). CBT focuses on challenging cognitive distortions and changing automatic thoughts into more positive ones to help with daily life.

CBT can teach individuals new habits and ways of thinking so that they can relieve mental and physical stresses. It helps people learn strategies to deal with negative thoughts and emotions, it promotes productivity in life, and it builds confidence to help them deal with challenges in any given moment.

CBT is also a form of "talk therapy" and focuses on talking to a professional counselor of some sort to help you manage and cope with your negative thinking patterns. It is a process in which you frame and perceive your thoughts differently and handle the world around you with confidence instead of fear or other intense emotions. In other words, CBT is based on the idea that our thoughts influence our feelings, so changing the way we think about and react to situations will help us feel better.

Like DBT, you can learn how to implement CBT in one-on-one sessions or through group therapy. In these sessions, you may learn how to address certain life situations through role-playing activities. You will learn how to calm your mind, take control of fear, and make change. You may be asked to keep a cognitive diary to figure out the root of the problem and address your triggers. Finally, you will learn how to change your thought process and act accordingly in everyday life through learning skills of mindfulness and positive feedback.

Since CBT mainly focuses on present thoughts and beliefs, in some CBT sessions, you may experience looking into your past to figure out why you act and think the way you do now. CBT mainly focuses on cognitive behavior, so understanding how you think and replacing your intrusive thoughts with more positive ones can help the individual change how they perceive things.

What is the Difference Between CBT and DBT?

CBT and DBT are both two types of psychotherapy methods used to manage and cope with mental illnesses, and although they have similarities, they also have many differences.

CBT focuses mainly on talking to a specialist about problems and is also focused on people with common characteristics with regard to their thinking patterns. It helps people talk through and learn things like how our thoughts influence our feelings through emotional responses. Also, CBT is only used for a certain amount of time, until the individual learns how to cope on their own using the skills that they learned within the sessions. Cognitive behavioral therapy relies on cognition and rationale, which involves applying reason and logic to their thought patterns. This helps the patient understand how to respond to uncomfortable or challenging situations rather than letting their emotions take over.

DBT however, is a type of CBT but it focuses more on helping people acknowledge the pain and discomfort they feel resulting from their negative and intense emotions. They learn through DBT how to feel "okay" and safe in the moment when overwhelming emotions arise, and also learn to feel empowered and confident to make healthy behavior choices. CBT helps with depression, anxiety, PTSD, phobias, and OCD - obsessive compulsive disorder. It helps these individuals gain control over their thoughts, and challenges their negative patterns with healthier ones, DBT particularly helps with people suffering from borderline personality disorder, eating disorders, PTSD, and other extreme mood disorders. DBT focuses on teaching individuals how to change their behaviors, rather than just talking through one's issues. It helps patients respond effectively to their impulses and promotes understanding of feelings such as pain and rejection. In short, CBT acts as a talking method, whereas DBT focuses more on taking action and learning how to respond to behaviors in real life. CBT is more cognitive challenging, while DBT teaches you how to deal with emotional reactions.

So, what is the difference in the treatment methods? This question is simply answered by the very fact that CBT focuses on how your thoughts, feelings, and behaviors influence one another, and then how to challenge them by implementing more positive ways to approach your thinking. In cognitive therapy, you fix these unhealthy patterns by talking about them. CBT redirects thoughts and helps the patient find ways to accept themselves as a whole, manage their emotions effectively, and prevent harmful behaviors from taking place. Now, DBT is a more active therapy where patients will undergo sessions of learning about the four modules; mindfulness, distress tolerance, emotion regulation, and interpersonal skills. DBT is for people who have problems with actually acting out their urges for self-harm or experience recurrent trauma that doesn't go away from CBT treatment alone.

What is Borderline Personality Disorder?

Borderline Personality Disorder, also known as BPD, is a complex and serious mental illness. People with BPD have extreme difficulty regulating or managing their emotions and controlling their impulsive behaviors. They are highly sensitive individuals who can react inappropriately to small changes in their environment.

Someone who suffers from borderline personality disorder may show patterns of unhealthy or unstable relationships, distorted self-image, intense emotions, and impulsiveness. Usually, people with BPD have an intense fear of being abandoned and having instability in their life, which can stem from an intense fear of being alone. They can often push people away with their severe mood swings and anger issues or impulsive behaviors, although most sufferers desperately want the sense of security that comes from having loving relationships with others.

Other mental health problems that a person suffering from BPD may also suffer from:

- Major to moderate depression
- Substance abuse like drug and alcohol addictions
- Eating disorders such as bulimia, anorexia, or binge eating
- Addictive personalities, such as having an addiction to gambling
- PTSD
- Social phobia
- Bipolar disorder
- Anxiety disorders such as generalized anxiety disorder (GAD), obsessive compulsive disorder (OCD), and specific phobias like agoraphobia.

It can be difficult to diagnose someone as an individual with BPD due to the following other mental health problems that often coexist with borderline personality disorder. At times, the BPD may be managed effectively, but other mental illnesses, such as anxiety or PTSD, may flare up, which can cause a relapse in BPD symptoms. A pattern of relapsing might then begin.

BPD usually starts in the early adolescent years. Researchers have concluded that both genetic and environmental influences have a strong influence on developing borderline personality disorder. Traumatic events in early childhood may cause BPD, such as mental, emotional, physical, and sexual abuse. Neglect, narcissism, and bullying may play a role as well in the development of this mental health problem.

Symptoms of BPD

Symptoms of borderline personality disorder can differ from person to person. In general, the symptoms of BPD include the following:

- Short spurts of anger, anxiety, or depression
- Emptiness accompanied with feelings of loneliness and possessiveness

- Paranoid thoughts and dissociative states in which the mind shuts off or becomes "foggy" due to painful thoughts or flashbacks
- Changes in self-image depending on who the person is hanging out with
- Impulsive and harmful behaviors such as abusing substances, gambling, or having eating disorders.
- Non-suicidal self-harm such as cutting, burning oneself, or overdosing that can bring relief from mental and emotional pain
- Extreme fear of being alone, abandoned, or neglected
- Volatile or hostile interpersonal relationships due to moods that can shift from idealization to anger in a snap.

Treatment for BPD often includes dialectical behavior therapy, cognitive behavior therapy, schema therapy, system training for understanding emotions, transference-focused psychotherapy, and mentalization-based therapy. Although medication can reduce the symptoms, it has not been shown to completely cure the disorder. Some prescriptions are given to people that suffer from BPD, but usually only to help minimize certain symptoms like depression, psychosis, and paranoia. For some people, medication along with therapy is needed.

How Does DBT Help People with BPD?

Dialectical behavior therapy is essential in the recovery process for someone with BPD. Since most of the symptoms of BPD are what DBT concentrates on controlling, it would make sense that DBT is the best fit for helping people with BPD manage their condition. Someone who has the disorder will have a difficult time handling their emotional pain, and so throughout the four modules of DBT, the individual will undergo a series of four stages.

The individual will learn the four modules of DBT in various steps or stages. Each stage has a "stage goal" to help someone with BPD target their specific needs, and so they will work with a clinician in hopes of addressing their disorder as a whole.

In stage one, individuals with BPD will be equipped with tools to help them regain control of their behaviors. The goal of this stage is to remove unhealthy behaviors like self-harm, while helping the individual develop positive coping mechanisms to respond to their emotional pain.

In stage two, the goal is to help people fully address and accept their emotions. Since it is common for someone experiencing BPD to be unable to accept or address their emotions, it can be too easy for them to withdraw and shut themselves off, so stage two is beneficial for these individuals. With the self-sabotaging behavior an individual with BPD often engages in, they can easily push others away as well, leaving the individual completely isolated, which can worsen BPD symptoms. DBT gives the person the skills necessary for accepting a range of emotions without the fear of giving into their intense feelings or being controlled by them.

In stage three, the therapy focuses on teaching individuals with BPD to create an ordinary life while maintaining healthy interpersonal relationships. DBT gives individuals the skills needed to address complications and arguments with other people, like family, friends, and partners, as well as difficulties that arise in life and at work. Often this stage opens the door for emotional triggers to set in, which gives individuals opportunities to practice the techniques learned in stages one and two.

In stage four, the previous stages need to have been completed in full. People with BPD often feel lonely or empty and incomplete. In the fourth stage of treatment, DBT addresses these feelings and helps the individual feel connected or reintegrated with their environments. Encouragement through spiritual pursuits, changes in career ambitions, and strengthened interpersonal relationships make the individual want to develop a sense of meaning in their lives. Stage four helps greatly with this aspect of the recovery process.

DBT ends when the person with BPD has accomplished all of the stages and understands or proves that they can manage the world on their own. DBT is very beneficial for BPD because it allows the person to accept their emotions and feel closer to the people they love, while also addressing and working on their self-esteem issues.

In the following chapters, we will discuss in more detail how each module works, how to undergo DBT, and how you can benefit from the experience.

Chapter Two: Core Mindfulness

The first of the four modules of DBT is **Core Mindfulness**. But what exactly is mindfulness?

In a nutshell, it is the art of bringing your focus to the center of the here and now. When you are anxious, fearful, temperamental, emotional, or otherwise, mindfulness helps ground you by bringing you back to the present moment. It allows you to pay full attention to the very act of what you are doing right now. This means that you bring your awareness to your thoughts, bodily sensations, feelings, and the environment through understanding and gentle perception. Gentle perception is when you perceive things without judgment and you are kind with your thoughts, not thinking of them as good or bad, or labeling them to mean more than they do. Mindfulness is about watching these aspects carefully and being aware nonjudgmentally of what is going on with you in the current moment. It is to fully accept whatever is going on without determining if a feeling or sensation is "right" or "wrong." This helps people with borderline personality disorder or eating disorders because it helps center their attention on the present, rather than focusing on their mistakes of the past or their worries of the future.

Often times, people who struggle with the many disorders that DBT helps with, such as mood disorders, may find their minds spiraling and obsessing over things they can't control. They lose touch with themselves and may feel dissociated, which is a feeling of being "out of their body." Mindfulness helps with these symptoms by bringing the person's focus back to what's going on right now.

By being aware of the given moment, you can bring yourself back and ground yourself, which can stop a panic attack in its tracks and also help with recurring mood swings. Mindfulness is a type of meditation that you can do anywhere at any time, and with practice, it can help to minimize your symptoms immediately.

Often when people try to meditate, they focus too much on the benefits or the end result. Before trying any other types of meditation practices, it is best to start with and learn about mindfulness meditation, since mindfulness doesn't have an "end" result, it simply focuses on living in the moment. If you are too focused on what the end result is, your meditation practices will never go as planned. When you do practice meditation, just be "mindful" of the fact that the only thing you have to concentrate on is the second you are living in right now.

Mindfulness has several benefits: stress reduction, improved stress management, and performance enhancement. It can also help us with understanding both ourselves and others as well, which develops empathy and awareness of how our actions affect other people and our environment.

What You Need to Know About Mindfulness

The reason why mindfulness is so recommended even outside of DBT is that it helps unlock the instinctive curiosity levels of our minds. It also lets us accept ourselves and others without judgment.

Here are some more things you need to know about mindfulness:

1. **Mindfulness is not vague or unusual**

   Mindfulness is a practice we already have established inside ourselves and our minds. We do it instinctively all the time without being aware of it. For example, have you ever been so enthralled by a movie or by a conversation that everything around you didn't matter? This is a form of mindfulness. Or, have you ever just shut your eyes and paid attention to what your heart was doing? Maybe you noticed how fast or slow it was going. Or maybe you concentrated solely on your breath without changing it and you didn't observe any thoughts? Those are other examples of mindfulness.

2. **Mindfulness is not an added thing we have to do**

   Because mindfulness is so easy, we already know how to be completely present. It doesn't ask us to be different, and it doesn't change how the world around us moves. With the qualities of mindfulness, we can practice it anywhere, whether that be in our offices at work, while we are working, when we talk to others, or during anything we choose to take part in.

3. Anyone can do it

Mindfulness is universal which means that anyone can do it because it does not require change or an extra form of "brain power" or thinking. You don't need to change your perspective or beliefs to benefit from mindfulness.

4. It's the way to live

When people get really good at practicing mindfulness meditation, they can easily make it a way of life where drama, tension, and stress become a thing of the past.

5. It sparks creativity

The world around us is very complex and unpredictable, which can create worry for some people who have a hard time welcoming change or being a part of something they cannot control. Mindfulness helps us become resilient to life's seemingly unforgiving problems.

Often times, before we start meditating, we get so caught up in our minds worrying about how to meditate, when we are going to start, or how we are going to start. Sometimes, it may not actually have anything to do with the meditation itself, but about our lives in general. What we don't realize about mindfulness meditation is that, unlike other meditation practices, we actually need to focus on these thoughts that are spiraling inside our minds.

To begin mindfulness meditation, you need to create a sense of calm before actually meditating. This means to be completely aware and intentionally "fix" your breathing. To do this, you need to close your eyes, center your mind around your breath, and take a deep breath in while putting one hand on your stomach and one on your chest. Make sure that your chest is barely moving, and that your stomach is sucking in all the air. Once you inhale as much oxygen as you need, you hold this for a couple of seconds, then exhale everything out, still making sure your chest is not moving. Repeat this process until you feel focused and calm. Once you are breathing deeply into your stomach without having to consciously focus on it, you can now focus on your thoughts, your bodily sensations, and the environment around you.

Some things to ask yourself about your environment are:

- How cold is the air?
- Is there a breeze?
- Is the air still?
- What can I hear?
    - Traffic?
    - Music?
    - Talking?
    - Is it silent?
- What can I smell?
    - Is it fruity?
    - Musty?
    - Mildew?
    - Or nothing at all?
- What can I touch?
    - What does the surface I am laying on feel like?
    - Is it hard?
    - Is the ground soft?
    - Where am I?

Some things to ask yourself about your bodily sensations are:

- What are my feet doing?
- What are my facial expressions doing?
- What is every part of my body in between doing?
    - Do I feel tingly?

- - Do I feel cold?
  - Do I feel warm?
- Is my heart racing?
  - Is it normal?
  - How many beats do I think it is beating per minute?
- Am I hungry?
  - What is my stomach doing?
  - Do I have butterflies?
  - Are my stomach and gut completely still?
- What does it feel like when I smile?
- What does it feel like when I wiggle my toes or fingers?
- What exactly is happening to my body in this present moment?

Some things to think about when focusing on your mind are:

- Why do I feel the way I feel right now? (sad, happy, mad, irritated, confused, etc.)
- The past is the past, all I have is now.
- The future is untold, and I don't need to waste my energy on worrying about that right now.
- I am here.
- That's a strange thought, let's watch it to see how long it sticks around.

- That's an odd image, let's watch it to see how long it lasts.
- All I have is now, and all I am going to focus on is the here and now.

Remember during this process to remain as nonjudgmental as possible. Notice what is happening within and around you, but don't judge it.

Do you see the difference between being mindful about your environment as opposed to your own sensations? Do you see how both are very different from when you focus on your thoughts? When you bring your full attention to your thoughts, notice how you are not judging them or changing them. You notice them and let them stick around as long as they need. You aren't avoiding them, but neither are you labeling them. You are simply present at this moment with them. This is the very art of mindfulness.

History of Mindfulness

Mindfulness originated from Eastern philosophy and has been practiced for thousands of years. In the past forty years, western societies have taken up the practice.

Mindfulness began around 1500 BCE under the practice of yoga in the religion of Hinduism. It was implemented in Buddhism when practicing the focus of the breath in 535 BCE. Christian, Muslim, and Jewish religions practiced the art of mindfulness as well. Mindfulness in the modern age is now also used in clinical practices to help people with personality disorders, anxiety, depression, and chronic pain.

Jon Kabat-Zinn founded the Stress Reduction Clinic at the University of Massachusetts Medical School in the late 1970s. From this Stress Reduction Clinic, is where stress reduction through the "mindfulness-based stress reduction" (MBSR) program came about. This program was designed to help conditions such as chronic pain, heart disease, anxiety, sleep problems, and depression. Later, in the 1990s, Mark Williams, John Teasdale, and Zindel Segal developed MBSR to further help people with depression, by coming up with mindfulness-based cognitive therapy (MBCT). Which was clinically approved by the National Institute for Clinical Excellence (NICE) in the UK, as a treatment option for depression.

Whether mindfulness is used in religious or scientific forms, both practices are used to help meet emotional calmness, ease restless thoughts, and to help someone become more focused and aware of themselves and their surroundings.

Benefits of Mindfulness Practice

There are many benefits to being mindful; in fact, there are almost as many benefits to being mindful as there are to eating healthy and exercising. However, with mindfulness, instead of exercising your body, you are exercising your mind.

Mindfulness helps your mind stay in shape and the limbic system stay balanced. The limbic system in our brains is attached to the amygdala and hippocampus, which are responsible for sending signals to each other to produce feelings of anxiety and fear. By balancing the limbic system, we can focus better, plan more easily, and problem-solve more effectively. The most common benefits of practicing mindfulness are as follows:

1. A decrease in stress and anxiety

Stress and anxiety happen when we cannot focus our attention away from what is bothering us, or when we cannot stop overthinking and constantly worrying. The constant emotional baggage that keeps our muscles tense can also cause anxiety and stress. This is because surges of cortisol, a stress hormone, rush through our bodies and keep our minds racing while also sustaining chronic pain. Mindfulness is about turning our minds away from the anxiety by focusing on the moment and calming the cramped muscles we feel by reducing stress. Since what we think about is directly linked to how we feel, our goal is to change how we feel through changing our thoughts.

2. Enhanced concentration and focus

The main reason why most people have a hard time focusing or concentrating is that they have too much on their minds. Often, we procrastinate on tasks we need to do, which only puts more stress on the mind and body. We become easily distracted or lose time daydreaming, which are other forms of procrastination. Mindfulness helps by decreasing this short attention span, calming the mind, and allowing us to concentrate solely on what is important at this current moment.

3. Better interpersonal relationships

Many of us struggle with communication when developing a strong or close relationship with someone. This is mainly because everyone perceives life and their selves and environments differently. So, the best way to practice effective communication is to listen with your full attention before figuring out how to respond. You also need patience when waiting for the other person to think about what they are going to say before they respond. Mindfulness teaches us how to be patient and have open communication by listening effectively. It also helps us respond without judgment.

4. Promotes sleep

The main reason many people can't fall asleep or stay asleep at night is that their minds can't stop racing. This is because we don't have time in the day to think about the things that bother us, so our minds become wide awake at night. By being mindful of this and practicing mindfulness meditation (especially at night), we are giving our thoughts attention and taking note of them, which helps our mind calm down. Furthermore, mindfulness meditation can be very relaxing, which is perfect for helping you to fall asleep.

There are many more benefits you can experience after you practice mindfulness. But that's just it, only **after** you start making mindfulness a daily **habit** will you will start to feel these benefits. It's the same thing as practicing anything else; you won't actually feel benefits unless it's something you make a habit and stick with for a period of time.

So, you may be asking, how long will it take until I experience these benefits? Don't worry about that too much for now. Focus instead on creating the habit of mindfulness and take your attention away from any perceived benefits you hope to get. In no time, the benefits will arrive, and mindfulness will have developed into a daily activity that you cherish.

There are two things that you should aim for when trying to maintain a long-term mindfulness practice:

- You have to practice at least three to five days a week.
- Each practice needs to last at least twenty minutes per session.

If we practice mindfulness intermittently or once in a while without maintaining a set routine, then we won't get to feel the full benefits it brings. If we practice mindfulness for a while and then stop when we start to feel the benefits, the benefits will also drift away. It's like learning math and then forgetting it; we cannot stay good at something if we do not keep practicing it. So, to feel all the benefits and keep them in our lives, we must make mindfulness meditation a daily routine. Luckily, mindfulness is easy to do and won't take much work to get started. If you dedicate yourself to practicing mindfulness at least five days a week, if not every day for twenty minutes throughout the day, then you will be the most successful.

So, how do you get started? Although mindfulness is a simple task, it doesn't mean it's going to be easy to keep doing. Dedicating yourself to being mindful every day means that you have to implement self-discipline and stay on track.

Here are the steps to get you started:

Step One: Getting set up

Pick a set time or times when you are going to practice. Take a look at your schedule and see where meditating will be able to fit. Maybe it's on your lunch break at work, before bed, or before your coffee in the morning. Set aside at least twenty minutes each day and stick to it. Having multiple 20-minute sessions per day is only going to help you feel the benefits sooner, so if you have the time spare, then make the most of it. As you develop the habit of mindfulness, you will begin figure out which times of the day are the easiest or most beneficial for you.

Build up to twenty minutes. When you first start practicing mindfulness meditation, you probably won't be able to reach twenty or thirty minutes right off the bat. However, the goal is to build up to it as quickly as you can. For the first day or first few days, do five minutes every session. Next, do ten minutes when you are ready, and so on. Make it a goal that by the end of the week you will have twenty minutes of mindfulness meditation every session. The reason twenty minutes or more is the goal is that anything less than that per session will provide far fewer benefits.

Step Two: Starting the practice

What does mindfulness actually look like?

Sit down in a comfortable and supportive posture. Sit in a chair, on a couch, on the floor, or wherever feels the most comfortable. If you choose to, you can lay down, but make sure that you don't fall asleep. If crossing your legs feels comfortable, then do that.

Close your eyes and focus on what your breath is doing. What does your breath feel like? Focus on the sensations that are going through your body right now. Feel how the air fills your lungs and notice how cold or warm the air is. Focus on the cool sensation as it's going through your nostrils. The goal is to just sit with your breath and notice every sensation that comes along with it. In this practice, when you find yourself becoming distracted by your thoughts, simply bring your awareness back to focus on your breath. Don't judge yourself for losing concentration; it happens to even the most experienced meditators. Just accept that it happened and return to focusing on your breath.

Just breathe normally. Mindfulness meditation is not about intentionally changing your breathing habits, it is simply about watching how you normally breathe. The goal is to feel at ease and relax into yourself by intentionally paying attention to your breath. If your breathing was irregular or fast when you started, it should gradually slow down as you continue to focus your attention on your breath.

Step Three: Managing challenges

Some challenges may arise when you start out, like becoming distracted or focusing too much on your thoughts or being judgmental about yourself. Maybe you even feel weird about meditating at first; however, these are all normal things. It's not a race, nor is it a competition; it is just the art of being.

Accept that you will get distracted. When you notice your mind shifting, like wondering when the timer is going to go off or if you are doing it right, remember that it's okay. Move your attention back to your breath without staying on your thoughts for too long. It's normal to feel this way and think these things. It's almost necessary because you are rewiring your brain to shift from "thinking" mode to "awareness" mode. The whole point of mindfulness is to pay attention when you have become distracted and then to consciously shift your attention back to your breath.

As you carry on with your practices and meditation, you may feel as though some sessions are easier than others. However, almost immediately after you are done with each session, you should feel calmer and more at ease with a general sense of being more environmentally and personally aware. Remember though, these effects won't last if you don't stick to the habit. Don't judge yourself if you cannot finish a session or if your session didn't go as planned. By maintaining the routine, you will get better at it. Mistakes are normal, and if you don't make them, you won't learn.

Here are some takeaway suggestions to help you achieve complete awareness of the present moment when practicing mindfulness:

- Always focus on your breath, or on the sensations that are happening in your body.

- When your mind gets distracted, gently acknowledge this has happened and bring your focus back to what you were originally doing (your breath, your bodily sensations, etc.).

- Let your stomach expand fully while feeling the air enter through your nostrils.

- Notice each sight (if your eyes are open), touch, scent, taste, and sound while being intentionally aware of all your senses.

- Once you have your breathing down pat, you can broaden your awareness to what is happening around you or what is happening internally to you.

- When you have mastered the art of becoming aware of your surroundings (without being distracted), you can then focus on what your thoughts are doing. If they start racing, go back to the beginning by bringing your attention back to your breath.

Mindfulness Techniques

The absolute goal of mindfulness is to stay alert, focused, and relaxed at the same time, and develop a new sense of calm while letting go of everything else. What is most important is to always be in the moment. So, when your mind rehashes the past, focus on the now. When your mind races to the future, bring your attention back to your surroundings. Only the thoughts of what is happening today or right now should be welcomed. However, mindfulness is the art of welcoming and letting go of all thoughts as a whole, and as such there are other types of mindfulness that are designed to focus on specific things. The different types of mindfulness meditation are as follows:

- **Basic mindfulness meditation** - With this practice, you are only focusing on your breath. When you notice yourself shifting your attention to anything else like your surroundings or your body or your thoughts, shift your attention back to your breath. Allow everything else to come and go as smoothly as possible.

- **Bodily sensations** - This meditation is where you become mindful of every body-part that you have, starting from your toes and going through each part, ending with your head. If you notice a tingle or an itch or your heartbeat or pulsing in your head or anything else, just acknowledge it. Make a mental note and move on to the next body part. You do all of this while still controlling your breath, breathing slowly and steadily.

- **Sensory** - Sensory mindfulness is about becoming aware of the five senses (sight, sound, smell, touch, and taste). Name the colors around you, the smells you smell, the textures you feel, the sounds you hear, and the tastes you have. Notice each, and then let them go, moving onto the next sense.

- **Emotions** - Allowing your emotions to take place without judgment is the goal of this mindfulness technique. If you feel angry, simply acknowledge it, and move on. If you feel sad, acknowledge it, sit with it, and move on. Be completely aware of every emotion that passes through your body. Try not to name them as good or bad; just accept that you feel this way, and let it go.

- **Urge surfing** - This practice is used to help people who have addictive behaviors cope with their cravings. Notice the sensations, emotions, and senses you have when you are having an urge, and instead of wishing it would go away, just know that these feelings will subside. This practice is about understanding that the feelings you have now will not last forever.

In every mindfulness exercise you do, at least one of the above techniques will be practiced. The goal is to be able to practice at least one type per day. However, if you don't have urges or cravings, the urge surfing is not needed. The goal is to be aware and mindful of whatever is happening to you in your life and letting it go. This decreases a lot of the stress in your life and will get easier as you continue to practice.

Mindfulness Practices You Can Do Every Day

You can choose to sit with yourself and do twenty-minute sessions of mindfulness meditation at once, or you can choose to do it throughout the day in almost everything you do. However, choosing both methods is your best bet to get as many benefits as possible. If one day you don't have enough time to practice for a full 20 minutes, then the following exercises are perfect for you:

1. **Mindfulness walking**

    Exercising your brain through mindfulness meditation is essential; however, combining it with the habit of exercising will give you additional benefits. In this activity, walk for at least fifteen minutes to half an hour. This will get your blood flowing. Taking a walk in nature is usually the most relaxing; however, if this is not an option, walking anywhere will still work.

    Mindfulness walking is about paying attention to everything you see while also taking in the fresh air, scents, and sounds around you. Focus on your feet touching the ground and how your legs feel with the repetitive motion of walking. Then move on to how your stomach and gut feel, to your heartbeat, and chest. Move from there to the rest of your body parts while continuing to simply just notice what is happening as you walk. Once you are done paying attention to your body parts, focus on your breath, then move your focus to the world around you. What do you see? How do your surroundings make you feel? Label them and let them go. The goal is to reach a relaxed state while you're walking. Take your time and go at your own pace.

2. Mindfully eating

After taking a bite of your food or a drink of your beverage, intentionally focus on the taste and textures. What does it taste like? Is it spicy, sweet, or savory? Is it cold, warm, or hot? Chew slowly and savor every taste that enters your taste buds. You don't need to do this throughout the whole meal, just enough so that you are completely in the present with your food or beverage. Also, you can focus on other aspects of the meal like how the utensils feel in your hands or what the details on the cup are like.

3. Mindfully listen

Say you are having an extremely busy day. Emails are coming in, work is hectic, kids are playful and hyper, dinner is on the go, and you haven't even showered or had a chance to relax. Take a moment sometime in the day to just listen to what is going on around you. We can get so used to tuning sounds out, that we forget the importance of sound. We all underestimate the importance of what sounds are happening around us. Take five minutes and just stop. Is there music playing? What song? Do you know it? Who sings it? When your mind trails off, refocus back to the song. Are there kids laughing or traffic in the distance? What are your kids laughing at? Take five minutes and really focus on the sounds around you; this will help center you and bring you back to the present moment.

4. Mindful attention to the small things

We often forget to pay attention to the small things that we do every day. This can be brushing your teeth, showering, changing your clothes, or cleaning the house. Whatever it is, be mindful in these moments. For example, if you are brushing your teeth, pay attention to the taste of the toothpaste. Is it really minty or mild? Notice the bristles moving along your teeth. Notice the sound that your brush makes when you stroke back and forth. Feel your senses and pay attention to how you feel as you brush your teeth. Perform every chore and all the small things you do mindfully.

5. **Candle meditation**

Make the room dim, and light a candle. It can be any candle, whether it's a scented or unscented one. The choice is yours. Sit in front of the candle and be completely one with this candle. Look at it as if is the first time you have seen fire or a small flame. What color is it? How hot is it? Does the candle smell? Where did it come from? The goal is to not really do anything, just to look at this candle in a pure and simple way. Notice the flicker of the flame and watch how it dances. When you find your attention moving elsewhere, gently bring your attention back to the candle.

These exercises are just quick things you can do to practice being mindful. The more you practice, the better you will become, and the more benefits you will notice. DBT will teach you other methods of mindfulness and how to be mindful; however, this is a quick beginner guide on how to get started. If you are ready for a more advanced mindfulness practice, look into yoga and watch guided videos on how to be more mindful while simultaneously doing yoga. This combines a challenging physical activity with training your mind to stay present in the moment.

Chapter Summary

You now know that mindfulness is effective in helping with a variety of disorders and is practiced through each individual module. It doesn't require much thought (in fact no thought at all), and it shouldn't act as a burden because it requires no change in what you do. In fact, it's all about making the time to meditate mindfully each day. This benefits an individual greatly because we don't often pay much attention to our thoughts, motives, values, feelings, sensations, or our environment.

A lot of people "do" rather than "think", or they think too much about non-important things. Mindfulness helps someone notice these aspects about their thought patterns. It brings them back to the moment so that the future doesn't seem so bothersome and the past doesn't seem to have as much impact on the now. Being mindful of what is happening now as opposed to not being mindful at all will greatly improve your awareness of what is going on around you.

Of course, like most new things we challenge ourselves to do, it will take practice and dedication. However, with the right mindset and a positive attitude, mindfulness will become as instinctive as eating, brushing our teeth, and other habits we develop in our daily lives. The goal is to have mindfulness become habitual in order to gain the most benefit from it.

Chapter Three: Distress Tolerance

Distress tolerance is one of the core components of DBT.

This skill is designed to help you manage extreme emotional stress without acting in a destructive way. The main purpose of distress tolerance is to stop you from acting on the urges associated with your emotions. The goal isn't to get rid of or decrease the emotional pain and distress you feel. The goal is to tolerate and acknowledge it without reacting negatively.

When you are at a point in your life where you cannot handle something you are faced with, this can cause stressful feelings. This could be a break-up, the death of a loved one, or an unexpected accident. When this happens, distress tolerance skills are highly beneficial.

In short, distress tolerance skills are learned for when it becomes challenging to change something that is going on in our lives that causes distress. It is used as a coping skill (or mechanism) to survive a crisis and teaches us how to tolerate short-term and long-term emotional or physical pain.

Since DBT is mainly focused on helping people with borderline personality disorder, distress tolerance skills tend to focus on impulsive behavior, which is a symptom of BPD. This impulsive behavior means that they often have issues with drug and alcohol abuse, overspending, irresponsible driving, violence, and impulsive sexual behaviors.

In most cases, impulsive behaviors are triggered by intense emotions that the individual has a hard time controlling. Usually, it happens in this order:

1. A crisis happens, which triggers an extreme emotion. For example, the person experiences rejection, which results in depression or rage.

2. The feeling becomes so intense the individual feels as though they cannot handle it.

3. In an attempt to reduce the emotion, the individual turns to impulsive behavior, like drinking alcohol or driving fast.

4. The individual feels better but only for a short amount of time.

5. After the temporary relief subsides, the individual realizes two things:
    a. The trigger that made that strong emotion happen has not disappeared.

b. Because of what the individual did to get rid of their emotions, like drink excessively, they now feel another intense emotion of shame or guilt.

Distress tolerance skills learned through DBT help with handling triggers and the uncontrollable feelings that accompany them. They help the individual learn how to deal with intense emotions appropriately so that the impulsive behaviors don't occur. These skills give them alternative ways to react to triggers and help them recognize that their instinctive patterns are unhealthy impulsive behaviors.

Distress tolerance involves a six-skill program to be followed; however, there are two important strategies to learn about as well: acceptance skills and crisis survival skills. The acceptance skills involve accepting yourself and the situations that you are in that seem uncontrollable. The crisis survival skills involve you and your coach or counselor finding ways to tolerate in-the-moment feelings without acting on them and creating more problems. The goal behind learning these skills is learning to accept that feelings of pain and distress are a normal part of life. If you avoid or run from your pain and the feeling that a certain situation triggers in you, then you will only gain more pain and suffering. You must learn to accept that bad things are bound to happen and that, even though there is nothing you can do about it at times, there are healthy ways to manage the emotions that these situations cause.

Acceptance Skills

Many people have a hard time accepting things for the way they are, especially when outcomes turn out to be particularly far from our hopes and expectations. We typically do not reach acceptance because we have not gotten what we wanted, our circumstances have not turned out the way we expected, and we have been confronted with a situation that is scary and seemingly unbearable. DBT acceptance activities teach ways to become more accepting and understanding of reality. These functions or activities involve deep breathing, awareness exercises (mindfulness), and half-smiling exercises. The acceptance module of DBT includes the concepts of radical acceptance, turning the mind, and willingness. Instead of trying to change your reality to be how you want it, the acceptance module teaches individuals how to respond to a situation in a healthy way and accept the situation as it is.

Crisis Survival Skills

Crisis survival skills are skills to help you get through a crisis without acting on your impulses and making matters worse. These skills enable you to get through a difficult crisis in the calmest way possible. There are four sets of skills associated with crisis survival: distracting, self-soothing, improving the moment, and thinking of pros and cons. The benefits of learning these skills include reducing the distress caused by the situation at hand, becoming more kind to yourself through self-care, effectively being able to handle a crisis, and keeping you motivated to persevere throughout the process of dealing with a crisis.

Before we define exactly what distress tolerance is, let's break it into two parts and look at the singular words – distress and tolerance.

What is Stress?

There are two types of stress; distress, and eustress. Eustress is beneficial stress, such as the stress your body is placed under during a workout. Distress on the other hand, is negative stress. Sadly, this is the type of stress people are most familiar with. Stress develops over time and is a state of emotional or mental strain resulting from continuous problems or demands that life throws at someone. Distress is defined as 'an emotion we feel resulting from extreme anxiety, sorrow, and pain'.

There are different types of distress a person may encounter, with the three main ones being "acute" stress, "episodic" stress, and "chronic" stress. They each have their own symptoms, duration, and treatment. Understanding each of these will help us understand more about the distress component of distress tolerance.

Acute Stress

Acute stress, simply put, is the type of stress we feel as a result of worry. This acute stress is usually due to the pressure we have put ourselves under in the past, or the worry that develops from thinking about the future. Acute stress can be exhilarating, and exciting; however, too much of this can result in becoming overwhelmed or run down. For example, planning a road trip can be super exciting; however, if you worry too much about what might go wrong and obsess over thoughts such as "what if the car breaks down", you'll begin to feel overwhelmed.

Acute stress is the result of little things that happen in life. The build-up of these little things adds more and more pressure until it becomes too much to handle. Acute means short or brief, like when a part of your car breaks but it's easy to fix, having a deadline on an assignment, or experiencing a family emergency. Due to acute stress being short-lived, it doesn't actually do much long-term damage; however, the symptoms associated with acute stress can be worrisome.

Here are some of the common symptoms of acute stress:

- Emotional distress including anger, irritability, anxiety, and depression.

- Muscle problems like tension headaches, back pain, pulled muscles, and tendon or ligament problems.

- Heartburn, acid reflux, gas, diarrhea or constipation, and irritable bowel syndrome.

- An increase in blood pressure, increase in heart rate, sweaty palms and feet, dizziness, migraines, cold chills, chest pain, shortness of breath, and panic attacks.

As you can see, the above symptoms can be quite serious. Fortunately, acute stress comes and goes and is easily manageable.

Episodic Acute Stress

This is when acute stress becomes so excessive that there is too much going on at once, all the time. You are always on the go, always late, and always worried about things going wrong. You may feel as though you are always in a hurry, that you have too many errands to run, or that there isn't enough time in the day to do everything. With this perceived lack of time, things quickly pile up for the next day, which means you are always behind. It can feel as though you can't sit and breathe for five minutes, and when you do, even that seems rushed.

The symptoms resulting from this "go, go, go" life of over-arousal include; having a short temper, being on edge, constantly feeling tense, experiencing anxiety attacks, and feeling stressed all the time. Due to the hostile behavior that often results from episodic acute stress, interpersonal relationships are hard to maintain. Also, the workplace can become a very stressful place for people experiencing episodic stress.

"Worrywarts" also often develop episodic acute stress, because they constantly worry and obsess or overthink things that are entirely out of their control. They typically think negatively, don't see the optimistic side of things, and always see a disaster heading their way. These types of people are often in a hurry and live in fast-paced environments. They bring this stress upon themselves through their lifestyle and thought patterns.

The symptoms associated with episodic stress include:

- Constant tension headaches
- Migraines
- Hypertension
- Chest pain
- Heart disease

It may take many months for someone with episodic acute stress to find the right treatment for them. Effective treatment usually requires a specialist or therapist to help someone minimize their stress until it reaches a manageable level. Oftentimes, people don't see their stress as a problem because they have developed a routine or habits around this type of lifestyle. Until a person can admit that their stress is a problem, it will be hard for them to improve. Treatment requires a person's full effort and commitment to be effective.

Chronic Stress

Chronic stress is quite unlike acute stress, with the main difference being that acute stress can at times be thrilling or exciting; whilst chronic stress is the exact opposite. This type of stress wears people down day in and day out for years on end. Chronic stress kills our minds, destroys our bodies, and decreases our performance in various areas of life. This type of stress is what people experience when they are living in poverty, or are trapped in a dangerous marriage, or feel stuck in a career they despise. Chronic stress occurs when a person develops the perception of being trapped with no way out of their situation.

Sometimes, chronic stress stems from early childhood if the sufferer experienced a traumatic event while they were young. Sometimes, chronic stress stems right from a person's personality and how they view the world around them. Sometimes, it's a combination of both. No matter the cause, recovery from this type of stress comes from within and with the guidance of a professional counselor or specialist. The worst effect of chronic stress is that people begin to accept their stress as an unchangeable part of life. At this point, they surrender to their stress, and can become depressed, destructive, nihilistic, and even suicidal.

The deadly symptoms of chronic stress are as follows:

- Suicide
- Violent behaviors
- Impulsive behaviors
- Heart attack
- Stroke
- Cancer

People get so worn down from the pressure and demands of their lives that they feel as though there is no escape and have fatal breakdowns. Physical and mental resources become diminished as a result of long-term exhaustion.

What is Psychological Distress?

Psychological distress is the same thing as distress, but with a few small differences. Simply put, distress is the overwhelming feelings and emotions that impact your way of life and how you think. People with borderline personality disorder or other mood disorders may experience higher levels of distress than usual. A person who doesn't suffer from these types of disorders may handle a situation such as moving to a new house with a normal amount of stress, but someone who suffers from a mood disorder of some kind may become highly distressed by the situation. People that have these intense feelings are experiencing psychological distress.

Psychological distress is an unpleasant occurrence that affects your ability to complete daily functions. It can result in negative perspectives or views of the world, other people, and your own self. Distress is subjective to each individual as no two people see or experience things the same.

A person's susceptibility to psychological distress may stem from traumatic past experiences, which can result in a person struggling to respond appropriately to stressful events.

Other causes of psychological distress include:

- Medical illness
- Divorce, becoming a widow, or separation
- Starting a new career
- Being a victim of abuse
- Infertility or complications with pregnancy
- Mental illness

One person is not the exact same as another when it comes to distress. For example, if two people were in the same car accident, both may suffer from an oversensitivity to distress as a result. However, one may experience long-term distress effects, whereas the other person may just feel this distress for a short period of time before moving on.

Some symptoms of distress are as follows:

- Weight gain or loss
- Temperament or irritability problems
- Extreme mood swings
- Obsessive thoughts or impulses
- Unexplained physical illnesses
- Decreased pleasure in activities that are enjoyable or used to be enjoyable
- Hallucinations
- Headaches
- Delusions
- Reckless behavior
- The assumption that others are "out to get you"
- Feeling spaced out or that your thoughts aren't yours

Along with many others, these symptoms are the things that distress can cause when it's left untreated. This is another reason why DBT is so important, as it can teach you how to effectively manage stress and avoid these negative outcomes.

Six Skills Associated with DBT

We all experience some sort of trauma or unwelcome problems in our lives like the death of a loved one, or divorce. These things require what is called crisis survival, and DBT helps you to manage each life "crisis." When you undergo the six skill modules of DBT, you will better understand how to deal with life's complications and how you feel about them. Thus, you will be left making happier, calmer, and more positive responses to negative situations than what your original instincts might encourage you to make. By learning the six skills associated with DBT, you will help yourself feel better while simultaneously retraining your brain to act against your impulses and make smarter decisions needed to live a healthier and longer life.

The six skills are TIPP, ACCEPT, IMPROVE, PRO and CON LIST, SELF-SOOTHE, and RADICAL ACCEPTANCE

Here, we will go through each skill in detail so that you can better understand the different ways in which DBT works:

TIPP

TIPP is an acronym for Temperature, Intense exercise, Paced breathing, and Paired muscle relaxation. This skill is used when you have hit your breaking point, or rock bottom. This skill helps to bring you back from intense emotions and feelings of breaking down.

1. **Temperature**

   Temperatures in our bodies rise or fall when we are under a great deal of distress. If you feel too hot, you can splash cool water on your face, or eat ice cubes, or suck on a popsicle. When you cool down your body temperature, your emotions will cool down as well. It's the same idea as switching your situation or surroundings when you are under a ton of stress or have anxiety-like symptoms.

2. **Intense exercise**

   Exercise increases the oxygen levels in your body, increases blood flow, works off excess energy, and releases endorphins into the bloodstream. So, when feeling distress, do some exercise. This could be lifting weights at the gym, sprinting down the road in short spurts, doing jumping jacks, or even a few burpees until you tire yourself out. Anything that makes you break a sweat will do the trick! By doing this, your stress levels will decrease, and you'll feel more at ease than you were before you started your workout.

3. **Paced breathing**

   Slowing your breathing is a great way to calm down. By controlling the way that you breathe, or just noticing your breath, you will find that your emotions become easier to handle as well. There are many different techniques for how to slow your breathing and bring yourself to a relaxed state. However, a good one to try is box breathing, as detailed below:

   a. Take a breath in for a count to four.
   b. Hold for four seconds.
   c. Breathe out for four seconds.
   d. Hold for four seconds.
   e. Repeat until you feel calmer.

4. **Paired muscle relaxation**

   This technique is often taught in mindfulness and other meditative practices. This is the art of intentionally tightening a muscle group such as your calves and then releasing the muscle, while at the same time exhaling all your breath. Tighten each muscle group for five seconds while you hold your inhaled breath. This will show you the difference between being tense and relaxed and will make you aware of the places in your body that are holding tension. After each muscle group from your head and shoulders to your feet and toes are complete, you should feel much more relaxed.

The goal of TIPP is to get you out of your emotional and distressed mind and into the wise and rational mind. Following TIPP will help you make wiser and more logical decisions, rather than acting irrationally out of emotion.

ACCEPTS

ACCEPTS is an acronym for Activities, Contributing, Comparisons, Emotions, Push away, Thoughts, and Sensations. This is a group of skills that will help you cope with negative thinking patterns associated with distressing emotions. The goal of ACCEPTS is to keep your emotions in check until the problem you are facing becomes resolved.

1. **Activities**

    This part of ACCEPTS aims to distract your mind by focusing it on something else. This can be anything from reading a book, to making food, to going for a walk, or even drawing a picture. Try to become totally engrossed in whatever it is that you choose and continue until your mind feels more at ease and not so overwhelmed.

2. Contributing

Contributing means to contribute to the society or community through volunteer work or just by going out of your way to help someone out. It is a proven fact that when you do something kind for someone, you will actually feel emotionally and physically better. You could also knock out the first two acronyms with the same stone, since the activity you choose to distract yourself with could involve helping others. Some ideas are to help cook dinner, clean someone's house, move or organize someone else's place, or mow their lawn.

3. Comparisons

By comparing your life and your problems to someone else's life and problems, you will you gain a better perspective of your situation. Is a loved one or someone you care about going through a more difficult time than you? If they can get through their struggles, then maybe you can learn from their strength and overcome this uncomfortable feeling you have. Another way of looking at comparisons is to look at your past experiences. Have you been through worse? If so, then that means you got through it and can get through this as well, which will give you strength, motivation, and inspiration to not give up.

4. **Emotions**

   If you are feeling restless or have developed an intense feeling of sadness, anger, or fear that you can't seem to control and it's only getting worse, then try meditation for fifteen minutes. You can go back to the mindfulness chapter and practice one of those techniques. Feel what your feeling without judgment and let whatever happens happen. These feelings will not kill you, and you will only make them worse by avoiding them.

   Another option is to provoke the opposite emotion of what you are feeling. So, if you are sad, think of a happy time in your life, or watch a funny movie. If you are angry, you could focus on writing about a positive memory. By doing this, you may not feel completely better, but the intensity of your distress will not seem as extreme as it was before.

5. **Push away**

   It is unhealthy to do this for a long time or as a solution to your problem, but if you absolutely cannot handle how you are feeling, push it away for the time being. Distract yourself with something else, as stated in the first acronym of ACCEPTS, but only until you feel calmer and ready to decide how you will resolve your problem. As long as you set a time to come back to the issue at hand, pushing away can be a helpful strategy.

6. Thoughts

One thing is certain: Thoughts are always going to be there. It's important to recognize that your thoughts do not control you or how you act; only you can control your actions and behaviors. When your mind overwhelms you with intrusive and negative thoughts, challenge them or replace them with something else, like singing the alphabet backward. Do a crossword puzzle or something that will get your mind off of the negative thoughts and focused instead on something more productive that exercises the brain. This helps you avoid self-destructive patterns or self-sabotage until you are better able to manage and achieve emotion regulation.

7. Sensations

This part of ACCEPTS teaches you to rehash what you learn in mindfulness – to use all five of your senses. It's a self-soothing technique designed to ground you and bring you back to the present moment, rather than focusing on your emotions. When you practice this technique, you might like to try a warm bath with a bath bomb, while listening to relaxing music and dimming the lights. Pay attention to every sensation that develops in your body and be mindful of them. Other things you could do include taking a walk in nature, or simply sitting still and observing all of the details and sounds around you. Make sure that with anything you do, you practice focusing on exactly what you are doing, and the details of everything around you.

ACCEPTS teaches you how to take your focus away from the distressing emotions that are trying to take over. By following the steps in ACCEPTS, you will learn how to not become overwhelmed by your emotions through using a variety of distraction and calming techniques.

IMPROVE

No matter what, in life we will inevitably come across things which we cannot control. Techniques within IMPROVE will help you accept that you have no control over certain situations and assist you in making it through intense distress until the situation or emotions subside. IMPROVE is an acronym for Imagery, Meaning, Prayer, Relaxation, One thing at a time, Vacation, and Encouragement.

1. **Imagery**

    Imagery consists of imagining that you are successful in the future. It required you to imagine yourself feeling at ease, in control, and using your logic and wisdom to achieve your goal and overcome your problems. You play the future out in your head scene by scene, emotion by emotion. By practicing imagery, you may actually be able to act this out in a real-life situation. The goal is not only to improve the outcome, but also to imagine yourself successfully overcoming your problems, whether they are out of your control or not.

2. **Meaning**

    In every situation you are in, ask yourself: What can I learn from this experience? What do I want to learn? How can I achieve what I want? Maybe you want to be more understanding of others, maybe, you want to build closer relationships with your loved ones, or maybe you want to practice personal growth. Find a lesson you can learn in every experience and look at this as the positive aspect of an otherwise negative situation.

3. **Prayer**

It's like the saying "give your problems to God." You don't have to believe in a higher power or in God, per se, to do this. All you need to do is talk about your problems, and then let go of them. You can give the problems to God if that's what you believe, and if not, leave the problems for the universe to sort out. Simply verbalizing your issues and having faith that everything will work out can really help in managing your stress.

4. **Relaxation**

When we are stressed, a hormone called cortisol gets released into our system, and we become adrenal heightened and have fearful symptoms which cause us to tense up. This is called the instinctual "fight or flight" mode. To calm yourself, or to stop this hormone from getting out of control, do something relaxing or something you like to do that will keep you in a relaxed state. This could be yoga, guided meditation, reading a book, listening to calming music, a hot bath, or going on a nature walk. The goal is to relax your mind and body, and escape the feeling of a fight or flight situation.

5. **One thing at a time**

   This exercise aims to put you completely in the moment, practicing one moment at a time, and one thing at a time. Let go of the past and accept that you cannot control the future. Just focus on the now. Find one thing, and one thing only, and put 100% of your focus into doing that. Focusing on just one thing at a time will help you to avoid becoming overwhelmed. It can take practice to be able to effectively quiet the mind and remain focused on just one task, but it is well worth it. When you're able to focus on just one thing at a time, the mind has a hard time concentrating on the intense emotions, which then makes your feelings become less consuming.

6. **Vacation**

   Vacation means to take some time away from home and go on a much-needed break from all your problems; and have fun doing it! However, this vacation doesn't need to involve any actual travel. The vacation skill of IMPROVE involves visualizing yourself taking a vacation. Imagine a "safe" place and put yourself there. It could be in the mountains, by the beach, or in a meadow full of flowers or tall grass. The goal of a mental vacation is to relax your mind so that your intense feelings or emotions are easier to handle, if not completely gone by the time you come out of this visualization.

7. **Encouragement**

    This skill teaches you self-care and how to give yourself kindness. You don't always have to get encouragement from others; you can encourage and motivate yourself through inspiring affirmations. Create positive mantras and repeat them when you become overwhelmed, like: "I got this," "I am okay," or "This is an opportunity to improve myself."

The skills you learn with IMPROVE can be used anywhere and at any time. So, when you are faced with a big problem, or even a small one, and you start to feel your emotions getting the best of you, remember to practice one of these exercises. The more you practice, the better you will get, and you may even find that you have a "go-to" skill you like the best.

PROS AND CONS

The pros and cons skill of the DBT training does not have an acronym like the rest of the skills. Instead, it is exactly as you see it. You write or think about the pros and cons of a situation, and the possible solutions you can implement. This can help you make logical and reasonable decisions when you are not in your wise mind. Weighing out the pros and cons of every situation may help you visualize different outcomes and will help you understand the consequences to your actions and impulsive behaviors.

If you have urges to self-harm or become self-sabotaging while in a distressed mood, a pros and cons list will help you refrain from the urge. It will also help you decide whether to act on the urge or to tolerate it. Whether you make a mental note of a few bullet points, or you actually engage in creating a chart on a piece of paper, the benefits of a pros and cons list are endless.

SELF SOOTHE

Just like the skills in ACCEPTS, using your sensations as a way to self-soothe is beneficial for calming your emotions in a stressful situation. This can quickly reduce the negative thoughts and sensations that are establishing themselves throughout your mind and body. There are six self-soothing methods to learn when developing this skill: sight, hearing, taste, touch, smell, and movement.

1. Sight

Out of all our senses, sight is perhaps the one we take the most advantage of. When going through the different sensations in your body, go back to the mindfulness techniques and pay attention to the full detail of everything you see. Start off small, and gradually add more things to your list. For example, try to spot and label everything that has the color blue or green in it. Or name five things in your field of vision that remind you of something happy. Whatever you focus your vision on, pay full attention to every detail of what you see.

2. Hearing

Close your eyes and listen to sounds. Listen to something as far out as you can hear; this could be the traffic outside, or your neighbor's loud TV. You can also try listening to something closer, like listening to a new song and really focusing on the lyrics. A good exercise is to listen to a song on repeat, and with each time you play it you focus on a different aspect of the music. The first time, you could listen intently to the lyrics. The next time could be the drumbeat, and after that, the guitar. This can be very calming while also giving you a new appreciation and understanding of the music you love!

3. Taste

What is your favorite taste? Is it spicy, sweet, savory, sour, or juicy? Whatever it is, find something of this taste, and eat it. Feel the flavors bounce around in your mouth and try sucking the flavor out of it completely, savoring every bit of it. This can really help to direct your focus on what you are doing instead of the emotions you may be feeling.

4. Touch

Practice touching things that are close to you and name or label the texture. What type of material is it? If it's a hard surface, what is on this surface? How does a warm cup of tea feel in your hands? What does cold water feeling like running through your fingertips? Be completely in the moment with what you are touching.

5. Smell

Again, close your eyes and inhale deeply. What do you smell? Is it salty like the ocean? Fishy like seafood? Musty like an old house? Or can you smell food cooking? Can you identify the smell? Or have you become nose blind to the scents around you. If so, go to a different room and try again. Another exercise is to light a scented candle or put a few drops of your essential oils into a cotton ball. Hold it to your nose and pay close attention to how it smells.

6. Movement

DBT has introduced a sixth sense which is movement. Since your emotional state can be triggered by your physical movements, it makes sense that this would be added to the other five senses. Take a walk and feel what's really going on. Do a workout and pay attention to the muscles that are being used. Whatever activity you choose, give your full attention to the muscles you are moving in your body.

When self-soothing, go through each of your six senses and pay attention to only one at a time. This will reduce the intensity of what you are feeling and help calm you so you can switch from your emotional mind to your wise mind.

RADICAL ACCEPTANCE

Radical acceptance is when we have to make a choice about whether or not we are going to accept reality, or if we are going to try to control it. When we try to control it rather than accepting it, it can actually do more damage than good because of how our emotions are impacted. This is what radical acceptance teaches us. In time, as you start to understand acceptance, you will feel a sense of peace that will provide you with the strength to continue forward despite challenging circumstances.

Imagine that you fear going to the doctor because you fear that they will prescribe you with a medication you don't feel comfortable taking. You have an infection that has been developing in your body for some time now, and even though you know the smartest thing to do is to get antibiotics to fix the problem, you are worried about the potential side-effects of the medication. You may think to yourself that if you simply get lots of rest and eat a bunch of probiotic yogurt, the infection will subside. And maybe it will, but so far, it has only gotten worse. Radical acceptance is about accepting what needs to be done, regardless of the intense emotion behind the act itself. If you don't see the doctor, the infection might continue to worse, and you'll end up in the emergency room.

So, after some time of writing your pros and cons, you bite the bullet and go to the doctor. You get your medication, take it for the time needed, and walk away unharmed and completely free of infection. Even though you had a fear of going to the doctor, and a fear of what side-effects that taking the antibiotics might have, you were able to accept the situation and make the right choice. Radical acceptance is about accepting the intense emotions as they come, but practicing the skills implemented in DBT and overcoming the situation.

Chapter Summary

Distress tolerance is about coming to the conclusion that stress and emotions do not have to take over your life. It means realizing that just because you feel overwhelmed with distress and despair, it doesn't mean there is nothing you can do about it. Distress tolerance is more than just coping with your emotions; it's about learning to live with them even after treatment.

People with PTSD can greatly benefit from this module because unlike most other disorders, the main reason they suffer is that flashbacks and memories impair their ability to live healthily. Individuals with personality disorders, such as borderline personality disorder, can learn to turn distress into positive stress, called eustress. This module can help them understand that their behaviors can be changed consciously, and that they don't have to be under the control of their own emotions.

Chapter Four: Interpersonal Effectiveness Skills

Interpersonal skills are skills needed or used in everyday life when it comes to communicating and growing bonds with others. Socializing is human instinct and humans are the most social creatures in the world. As a result, interpersonal skills begin to be developed and improved upon from the day we are born. In a professional setting, interpersonal skills are used to understand exactly what encourages employees and co-workers, and how to get the most out of them. These are the skills we use when communicating with others both individually, and in groups.

Skills such as listening, questioning, interpreting, and understanding nonverbal communication are all abilities that contribute to one's overall interpersonal skills. Also, interpersonal skills can be focused around and developed from emotional intelligence, which has to do with understanding and managing your own and others' emotions. These skills are strongly associated with empathy.

Skills associated with interpersonal skills include:

- Effective communication skills
    - Verbal - what and how we say things.
    - nonverbal - body language and tone of voice.
    - Effective listening skills - How to interpret and perceive what others do.

- Emotional intelligence - managing your and others' emotions
    - Empathy
    - Awareness of oneself and others

- Being a team player - able to work with others formally and informally

- Compromise, influence, and persuasion skills - Being fully capable of making sacrifices and having a give and take relationship.

- The ability to resolve conflict - being able to come up with positive and healthy outcomes to disagreements through effective communication.

- Effective decision-making skills - the ability to make wise decisions regarding future and present problems.

Developing the above skills is vital when it comes to honing your interpersonal skills. Dialectical behavior therapy motivates and encourages someone to develop the interpersonal skills needed to function in their everyday lives. If we don't know how to work effectively in groups or if we are too selfish and unaware of others, then our performance in our careers will greatly suffer. Someone without interpersonal skills can come off as a narcissist, or as being non-empathetic of others; they can seem extremely self-centered, and their work life, personal life, and marriages would be negatively impacted. This is why DBT incorporates interpersonal effectiveness skills to teach people healthy, empowering ways to deal with difficult situations, as well as how to address others in a respectful manner, rather than being manipulative or passive-aggressive.

Someone with borderline personality disorder or some other form of a mood disorder may find it difficult to hold effective conversations because they only know how to act on impulse. Treatment through DBT teaches the individual how to maintain a close relationship, ignore subconscious impulses to engage in impulsive behavior, and balance priorities between wants and needs. DBT helps you build self-recognition, self-respect, and self-confidence.

In DBT, interpersonal skills are separated into three fields:

- Objective effectiveness - reaching the goal of interaction.

- Relationship effectiveness - succeeding in the interaction without conflict.

- Self-respect effectiveness - learning about emotional intelligence so that you can express your morals and boundaries while respecting the other party.

In order to accomplish these goals and pass the module, DBT implements four different acronyms to help the individual remember their training: THINK, FAST, GIVE, and DEAR MAN. These will be discussed in detail later in this chapter.

What is Emotional Intelligence?

Emotional intelligence, also known as EQ, is the ability to evaluate your own and others' emotions by labeling them correctly, and using them to guide your own thinking, behaviors, and influence. EQ allows us to connect with others on a deeper level, while also understanding ourselves better. Emotional intelligence has five main components:

- Self-awareness
- Self-regulation
- Motivation
- Empathy
- Social skills

Self-awareness is the ability to recognize and manage your own emotions. It is the main component of emotional intelligence because it greatly impacts other aspects like self-regulation, and empathy.

Self-regulation is the ability to address our emotions, then act on them appropriately. It is the ability to express your emotions by effectively communicating your needs. Self-regulation means the ability to regulate and balance your emotions as well as understanding how to manage them effectively in social settings.

Motivation in emotional intelligence means that we are able to motivate and inspire ourselves to move forward. It's not to motivate yourself to gain respect, wealth, or fame. However, motivation learned in emotional intelligence is more focused around motivating yourself internally which means that you are motivated to accomplish your own goals for your own personal reasons.

Empathy is when you are fully able to realize the emotions of others and act on them effectively. It's the ability to put yourself in someone else's shoes and address their concerns based on how you would feel in their situation. However, do not mistake empathy for sympathy. Just because you can feel empathy for others does not necessarily mean you can completely relate to them. You don't have to accept their behavior, take on their beliefs, or validate them. Empathy simply means that you can see their point of view and can consider a different perspective other than your own.

Social skills are the piece of the puzzle that tie the other skills together. When you learn self-awareness, self-regulation, internal motivation, and empathy, you can put all of it into play with your social skills. These are the skills that allow us to interact effectively with one another. Some important social skills to learn are effective communication, compromise, and decision-making.

Taking a closer look at emotional intelligence, here are some signs someone has a high emotional intelligence level:

1. **They have a wide emotional vocabulary.**

   Often times, we don't know exactly how we are feeling. We know that we are sort of feeling sad, mad, fearful, or indifferent, but struggle to put our exact feelings into words. Someone with a high EQ has specific words to describe exactly how they are feeling. So, if you are feeling sad, but you know you are actually in great distress with emotional heartache. Or if you are feeling mad but know that more specifically you are in a type of rage, and all you want to do is yell and throw a tantrum; you know exactly what you are feeling. When you develop your emotional vocabulary, you can address and communicate how you are feeling more easily. From there, you can search for positive ways through which to cope or deal with your feelings.

2. **Empathetic people stem from being curious about others.**

   Whether you are an introvert or an extrovert, you likely have a sense of curiosity about the people around you. Someone that holds a high EQ level may know how to read or analyze people and become very observant of their surroundings. Aside from that aspect, when they find someone who is feeling strong emotions, be it distress, or just being upbeat in general, they can easily sense the emotions that person is experiencing and relate to them.

3. Change is not scary.

Emotionally intelligent people know that things change, and most of the time it is out of their control. So, they develop a flexible schedule and are easily adaptable to their surroundings. They embrace change rather than fear it because they know that succumbing to fear won't help them adapt to the change at hand.

4. It's difficult to insult or offend an emotionally intelligent person.

It's hard to get under the skin of someone who is emotionally intelligent because they already have a firm idea of who they are. These types of people are confident, open-minded, assertive, easy-going, and understanding. Since they are in tune with their own emotions, they know if someone else tries to insult them it's because the other party has problems within themselves that they haven't fully addressed.

5. **They know how to say no and eliminate toxic people in their lives.**

   Emotionally intelligent people know when to say no because they know that taking on too much or saying yes to everything will only increase the amount of stress they experience. They also know that keeping toxic people in their lives is disadvantageous, so they will be quick to remove these people when possible.

You may find that emotionally intelligent people are assertive in getting what they want, hold strict boundaries, and don't tolerate being disrespected. This comes from the self-awareness in understanding with pure confidence what they deserve and what they don't. Having an emotionally intelligent person in your corner can be one of your best friends, and as you develop an emotionally intelligent personality, you will find things in life will come easier to you.

Effective Communication

Communication is something we use daily. Interpersonal skills are needed to develop effective relationships, as well as communication methods. You may be wondering why exactly communication needs to be effective.

The main reason why people do not have strong relationships is that their communication skills are lacking. We may say something or interpret what someone else says incorrectly, which then leads to conflict. Conflict happens when we don't listen effectively to the other person because we are so focused on what we are going to say next. Learning how to communicate can strengthen your interpersonal relationships, build trust and respect, and improve network strategies as well as decision-making and problem-solving skills. Learning to communicate is a fundamental component of interpersonal effectiveness skills.

Effective communication is about understanding the other person and their emotions as well as the intentions and influences behind the message that's being given. It's about the ability to clearly state your message as well as following and understanding the conversation as a whole. This requires an ability to understand and pick up on tones and body language, as well as listening with your full attention non-judgmentally. This way, both parties are completely heard and understood correctly.

Effective communication falls under four sets of skills:
- Listening with full engagement
- Nonverbal communication
- Managing and dealing with in-the-moment stress

- Being assertive in a respectful manner

Anyone can develop these skills, but it is best if you can learn to implement these communication skills in a spontaneous, on-the-spot manner. For example, speeches are more enjoyable when they are spoken rather than read word-for-word. The more you practice your communication skills, the easier and more instinctive communicating will be, making you a much more enjoyable person to be around.

Let's take a closer look at the four different skills needed to practice effective communication:

Listening with full engagement

Communication is more about listening than it is about talking. We should focus less on what to say and more on how to respond. Sometimes, not saying anything is your best option. Listening effectively is about understanding the meaning behind the other parties' words; it's about understanding the emotions behind the message that is being conveyed.

Listening and hearing what someone says are two very different things. When you listen, you are listening to everything that is being portrayed emotionally, physically, and mentally. When you just hear someone speak, it means that you may be distracted with other things, not being completely engaged in the conversation.

Here are some tips for developing an engaged listening technique:

1. **Completely focus on the speaker**

   Put all distractions away, like your phone, turn the music down, and shut the TV off. Engage in the conversation with no other distractions so that you can give the conversation your undivided attention. This shows the other person that you're interested in what they have to say and makes it easier to pick up on their nonverbal cues.

2. **Avoid interruptions or talking about yourself**

   When you redirect the conversation to yourself, it may make the other person feel as though you aren't listening. Also, it sends the message that what you have to say is more important than what they have to say, which is not effective listening.

3. Show interest

If you have no reason to interject, you can nod and occasionally say "mhm" and "okay." This shows that you are listening and encourages the speaker to continue. Make sure to smile and have an open and inviting posture.

4. Listen non-judgmentally

When you engage in conversation, you may not be able to relate to them or find what they are talking about very interesting. You don't have to share the same beliefs, have the same ideas, or like their values. However, in order to fully understand them and make them feel appreciated, you should let go of all previous notions about the person and listen non-judgmentally. So, let go of your inner criticism, and try to connect with the speaker instead of feeling negative emotions towards them.

5. Provide feedback

People like to be heard and understood, so paraphrasing back to them what you are hearing can greatly impact how the conversation goes. If you are following, they will say yes or try to get you to understand their point correctly by explaining things differently. And before you give your response, wait until they are completely finished talking. If you are unclear about something, before moving on to another topic, ask questions about what they meant.

Nonverbal communication

Nonverbal communication is about learning to use your body language as well as paying attention to the speaker's body language. Pick up on tones and attitude, as this can give you a clear idea about how someone is feeling and how you are portraying yourself. Body language includes facial expressions, movements, hand gestures, eye contact, breathing, and posture.

When you learn how to understand nonverbal communication, how to read it, and how to portray it, it will help you connect with others, express what you mean, and manage conflict in relationships.

Here are two ways you can read nonverbal communication:

1. **Be conscious of unshared differences**

    Take age, culture, religion, and emotional states all into account when reading body language from others. These may be different from you, and so it's good to take these into account when trying to build and grow interpersonal relationships. For example, a Canadian adolescent, a grieving widow, and a Japanese businessman will all use nonverbal cues and communication differently.

2. Look at nonverbal communication as a whole

Try not to center your attention so much on the single gestures or postures you see. Look at all the nonverbal signals, from eye contact to tone of voice as all encompassing. Sometimes, people can automatically cross their arms or instinctively roll their eyes, and it may not have anything to do with you or the way they are feeling.

Here are three ways you can *deliver* nonverbal communication:

1. Use words and nonverbal cues that match

It can be confusing not just to the speaker, but also to the listener if your nonverbal cues don't match with your words. For example, if you say you are fine, but your body language is closed off, you aren't making eye contact, and your tone is somber, your message won't be clear.

2. Use appropriate nonverbal cues when speaking to people

You wouldn't use the same tone or posture with a child as you would with an adult or a teenager, so keep in mind who you are speaking with.

3. Refrain from using negative body language

It can be hard to use positive body language, like keeping eye contact, if you aren't feeling very positive. However, when you act positive, a conversation can go a lot smoother if you just grin and bear it. For example, if you are preparing to speak in front of a large crowd and you are anxious or nervous, stand straight and portray yourself as confident. How we move has been shown to effect how we feel. Studies have shown that simply by changing your posture you can decrease stress hormones, while simultaneously increasing testosterone. So even if you're nervous, standing tall with your shoulders back won't just make you look more confident; it might actually make you feel more confident too!

Managing and dealing with in-the-moment stress

If you have ever said something out of anger or acted in an unfavorable way then regretted it later, it's because you were acting on impulse, which is usually a result of stress. By relieving stress, you can return to a calmer state and can avoid these regretful actions. When you are in a calm and relaxed state, arguments and communication will be smoother, so it's best to figure out the right time and place to have these conversations.

Here are some useful tools to stay calm when you are trying to effectively communicate:

1. **Use stalling tactics**

    If you need time to think, ask the speaker a question to help clarify their point of view before responding.

2. **Take a minute**

    Sometimes, it's best to just pause the conversation and walk away. Make sure to tell the other party this before walking out. Pausing to think and gather your thoughts can greatly impact the outcome of the conversation.

3. **Deliver your message clearly**

   What you say and how you say it are two very different things, but both are just as important as the other. Keep eye contact, maintain an appropriate tone, and speak clearly.

4. **Discuss a conclusion or end with a summary**

   It's not good to go on and on about problems and issues, so after delivering your message, make a finishing statement or have a finishing question. If your finishing statement leaves an awkward silence, be okay with this and stop the conversation there.

The best thing to do in a stressful conversation is to agree to disagree if all else fails. Make sure to compromise, and then take a moment to calm down. When things are going wrong, look for the positivity or humor in the argument.

Being assertive in a respectful manner

Being assertive helps to develop confidence, self-expression, and decision-making skills. Being assertive means that you are able to express your thoughts, feelings, needs, and wants in a polite and respectful way. Assertiveness means confidence and not being hostile, aggressive, or demanding. Effective communication is not about winning an argument or forcing opinions and beliefs. Assertiveness is all about understanding the needs of others, but also asking for your needs to be met as well.

To develop assertiveness, here are some tips:

- Value yourself and your opinions
- Know what you need and want
- Express your negative and positive thoughts
- Receive and give positive feedback
- Learn to say no

These tips speak for themselves in the fact that they are all important when striving to become more assertive. Understand that your negative feelings are natural, but they are no excuse for being disrespectful. Being assertive without showing respect isn't really assertiveness at all; it's rudeness.

By practicing these effective communication skills, you can build positive relationships around effective communication. If you follow the above strategies, you can improve your listening skills and overcome communication mistakes in the future.

DBT Interpersonal Effectiveness Skills

Dialectical behavior therapy teaches individuals how to grow strong foundations at the beginning of a relationship. The interpersonal skills learned help to maintain a healthy friendship, partnership, or other types of relationships. These skills are taught through the following acronyms: **THINK**, **FAST**, **GIVE,** and **DEAR MAN**.

For people who have not experienced healthy relationships throughout their lives, it can be difficult to understand what needs to be done in any given relationship. Any healthy relationship will require a lot of communication, the willingness to compromise and make sacrifices, as well as some give and take. The people who struggle to maintain healthy relationships are usually the ones who struggle with their moods. The interpersonal effectiveness module in DBT is comprised of these specific skills for people who have trouble maintaining a variety of relationships.

THINK

THINK was developed to reduce feeling distress caused by interactions with other people. When you are feeling upset or a negative feeling, this strategy will be useful when interpersonal problems arise. These problems can be a heated argument, an opinionated disagreement, or when you are unsure whether you should leave the room or not.

Think

This technique aims to help you understand why the other person is upset. Are they angry because they think you are being unreasonable? Are they sad because they are stressed? When engaged with someone who is upset, try to put yourself in their shoes and think about what might be causing them to feel that way. Think is all about looking at the situation from their perspective.

Have empathy

To be empathetic means to understand and feel the emotions of the other person. Why are they having these feelings? What is a good solution to solving the situation? What can you do to make them feel better while still getting what you want out of it too?

Interpretations

This step aims to help you understand why the other person did or said a particular thing. Were their actions and behaviors out of anger? Was it out of character? Try to be realistic when it comes to the problem and how they are acting. Is something else going on in their life that caused them to lash out? Did they have a stressful day at work? Or could it be as simple as that they're hungry, tired, and aren't thinking straight? These are all examples of things that could cause someone to act in a rude or unfair way towards you. Before reacting emotionally to them, take a minute to interpret why they might be acting the way they are.

Notice

Take note of the small things people do to try to make things better. Often, we are so caught up in our own emotions that we pass judgment too quickly or dismiss a person's intention of finding a solution. When you get like this, take a minute to walk away, before coming back to the situation to reevaluate. Does the other person seem scared? Are they upset, or angry? Would it be best to drop the argument and move on? Stop yourself from reacting emotionally by removing yourself if you need to, before returning to the situation and viewing things exactly as they are. If you realize that you were in the wrong, don't be afraid to apologize. Being able to admit when you're at fault will go a long way in developing and maintaining healthy relationships.

Kindness

Kindness teaches you to show the opposing party respect. It doesn't necessarily mean that you need to "kiss and make up" just yet. You can make it known that they hurt you and ask them to give you some space so you can cool off. Just make sure that you do so in a calm and respectful way and avoid personally attacking them. Being nice will encourage them to be nice back to you, whereas being insulting will likely have the opposite effect.

In the previous chapter, we learned about distress tolerance. Think of the acronym THINK as a distress tolerance skill, but use it in your interpersonal relationships.

FAST

With the skills under the acronym of FAST, it is best to use each skill in sequential order, and then all together. These skills focus on maintaining respect and positivity during a period of conflict.

Fair

When you are being fair, you are not judgmental, nor are you being dramatic or exaggerating when you speak. You aren't turning molehills into mountains; you are simply trying to be fair. Being fair includes both your thoughts and your actions. No matter how irrational the other person may sound, don't respond in kind. Be fair about the situation and strive to understand both sides of the argument.

(no) Apologies

Being apologetic is one of the main things that can make or break your relationships. It can do wonders for a relationship when you are apologizing in a genuine sense; however, if you apologize without changing your behavior, the apology will be meaningless. At the same time, you shouldn't have to apologize when you haven't done anything wrong, so don't say it just because you feel obligated to. Sorry is a word that should only be said when you truly mean it, and when you're ready to adjust your behavior so that you don't make the same mistakes again.

Stick to your values

Be honest with yourself about what you believe in. You should never second-guess your beliefs and morals. Set clear boundaries and stick to them. If you are unsure about what you value, then make a list of the most important things to you, and honor that list.

Truthful

Some questions to consider when being truthful are: Are you undermining the other person? Are you catastrophizing the circumstances? Is what you are saying true? Are you being true to yourself and the other person? Truth is not only about telling the truth to others, it's also about staying true to yourself.

Implementing these four FAST steps will allow you to maintain your dignity and should give you a sense that you acted appropriately.

The two skills we just covered — THINK and FAST — can be used during conflict. However, the next two skills — GIVE and DEAR MAN — are skills you can use in everyday interpersonal communication to maintain and grow healthy communicative relationships.

GIVE

The GIVE skill is appropriate in any circumstance, whether you are with a coworker, just meeting someone for the first time, or are with someone you have known for twenty years or more. It is effective in building and maintaining positive relationships.

Gentle

Gentleness is similar to being kind. When you are gentle in your approach to others, you come off as genuine and caring. It means to be mindful of how someone else is feeling. By being gentle, the person you are communicating with will feel loved rather than attacked. Your interaction will have a positive outcome if the situation or conversation doesn't feel hostile and no one is being defensive or feeling victimized.

Interested

Simply showing signs of interest when someone is talking will communicate to them that you value what they are saying, and that you care to know more. You can show interest both through your actions and through your body language (nonverbal communication).

Validate

You can validate what the speaker is saying by mirroring their body language and their emotions. Ask questions if you don't understand. For example, if they have said something you are possibly misunderstanding or misinterpreting, you would be wise to ask them to clarify their point.

Another form of validation can be that you are responding to their feelings. So, if they tell you that they're going through a tough time, you could respond with empathy, telling them something such as "I'm really sorry to hear that, I'm here for you if you need help."

Easy Manner

A large part of nonverbal communication is your posture. When interacting with someone, in order not to come off the wrong way, stay as relaxed and comfortable as you can. Sit with your arms open and maintain eye contact with the speaker. By doing this, you will seem more approachable and easier to talk to.

The GIVE skills teach you all about nonverbal and verbal communication tactics. By implementing the skills of GIVE, you will become more effective your communication in every relationship in your life.

DEAR MAN

The skills of DEAR MAN teach you how to ask for something in a respectful and effective manner. It doesn't mean that you will always get exactly what you want; however, it's about learning to be assertive. The skills should be used in order.

Describe

When you want to do something, start by describing the situation. For example, if you want to meet some friends for dinner, you could start by saying, "My friends are going for dinner at such and such a place."

Express

This is where you would say what you want, such as "I would like to join them for dinner."

Assert

This skill allows you to explain why what you want to do is important. Do this in a non-aggressive way while still being polite. You could say, "I haven't had the opportunity or free time to do something with them recently, so it would be really awesome if I could take this opportunity now to go."

Reinforce

When and if you get what you asked for, then make a reassurance to the person you're talking with. For example, you might say "I will make sure I clean the kitchen before I leave, and I won't stay out too late."

Mindful

Just like we explained and practiced in the second chapter, mindfulness is about being in the present. Do not focus on the past or the future. Don't worry about what might happen if you can't go to dinner, and don't worry about what your friends would say. Just focus on being in the moment when you are asking for what you want.

Appear confident

Whatever you are asking for, from whomever you are asking it, you must stay confident. Maybe you are scared to ask for a raise or are scared of being rejected. The person you are asking doesn't need to know exactly how you are feeling, so do your best to appear confident when you are approaching them.

Negotiate

If sometime during the request it seems as though the answer isn't going to be what you want, be flexible. Negotiate and compromise to find a solution that both parties are satisfied with.

Learning to ask for what you want in a respectful way can really have a big impact on your life. It's a good skill to have in the workplace when you need to request something from your boss, or when you are trying to negotiate a raise or promotion.

How to Apply Interpersonal Effective Skills

Interpersonal skills are very important but are often undervalued. Not having our personal needs being met can really affect our lives in negative ways. It can cause conflict, confusion, and tension. It can also be difficult for many people to reach out and ask for help from others. Learning interpersonal effectiveness skills and then using them in the real world can make it easier to ask for help when needed. Interpersonal effectiveness skills allow you to open up and be vulnerable with others when it feels scary to do so. These skills also enable you to confidently manage your relationships and interactions with others.

Interpersonal effectiveness skills are designed to work with the other skills covered in dialectical behavior therapy (emotion regulation, mindfulness, and distress tolerance) to help you ask for and get what you want. This is mostly because opening up, asking for what you need, and being assertive can be scary when it's never been done before. Learning and implementing any of the skills alone can be helpful, but they are most effective when all skills are developed together.

The easiest way to be effective when communicating and interacting with others is to focus on being mindful. This skill will help you take a step away from your emotions and your judgmental attitude and really pay attention to the other person. By paying attention, you will see others' needs as being just as important as yours, and you will be able to navigate a negotiation much better than if you weren't paying full attention. People like to see that you show interest in them, and so when you are being reasonable, respectful, and assertive, you will find that you have better interactions than when you're not paying attention or are acting impulsively.

Correctly applying interpersonal effectiveness skills will help you to make mindful and educated decisions in your relationships, and particularly during negotiations.

When dealing with another person, be it in a negotiation or just in day to day life, there will be times that you are required to make tough and important decisions. Before you make any final decisions, first consider the following set of questions:

Priorities

- Are my principles important?
- Does this relationship need to be fixed or mended in any way?
- Is my self-worth at risk?

- Will values and beliefs be damaged if I say "no" to what is asked of me?

Capabilities

- Am I confident that this person is the right person to give me what I need?
- Can I give them what they want?

Timing

- What is the person feeling right now? Are they mad or calm?
- Should I wait to request what I want, or do they seem as though they would say yes right now?
- Is this a bad time for me to bring up my request?

Homework

- How well do I know this person, or how familiar am I with this situation?
- Do I have everything I need to ask for this request?
- Am I completely clear about what I want and need?
- Do I understand their request clearly?
- Do I know 100% what I am about to say yes to?

Authority

- Does this person have authority over me?
- Do I have the authority over them?

Rights

- Would saying yes contradict my rights or morals?
- Would saying no contradict my right or morals?

Reciprocity

- Have I done for them what I am about to ask from them?
- Has this person done more or an equal amount for me than I have done for them?

Long-term vs Short-term

- Will letting go of the negotiation or request right now result in long-term problems?
- Will saying no result in long-term problems?

Respect

- Do I do anything for myself?
- Do I avoid appearing useless?
- Will saying no make me feel horrible about myself?

As you can see, making requests and negotiating or learning how to say no can be a big task and a lot to think about. So, before you ask something or say yes to something, take a long, hard look at this list of questions, as each answer you come up with will be very important and valuable to you.

The most unrealistic scenario would be a relationship where you always get your way and never compromise or play fair. This is where negotiation and compromise come in. Is there some way that you can both get what you want at the same time? Could one of you sacrifice something without losing out in the long run? What is truly non-negotiable to you? This is where you need to take a step back and look at your values and what you believe in. When possible, meet halfway. That way you will be better able to maintain a respectful and harmonious relationship at all times.

Also, mindfulness, when combined with interpersonal effectiveness, allows you to be in tune with yourself, the other person, and their feelings, as well as the circumstances you are in. It teaches you how to use your own experiences, your thoughts, and your emotions effectively and successfully to negotiate with others.

Another question you may want to ask yourself is what do you tend to focus on most? Some people focus on fairness, others focus on being right. If you focus too much on being fair when negotiating, that fairness might not be reciprocated by the other party and they may take advantage of your generosity. If you focus too much on being right, you may find that the other party begins to resent you and won't want to associate with you in the future. Instead, what you should be focusing on is the benefits that you will both experience, the enjoyment of the deal, and the respect you have for one another.

Chapter Summary

Interpersonal effectiveness is not just about other people and the way you behave in social settings. It's also about how to be assertive, how to negotiate effectively and fairly, how to communicate clearly, and how to develop and maintain healthy relationships. When you take on too much responsibility, you introduce stress into your life.

Stress is okay if it is in normal and healthy levels; however, stress can get out of hand very quickly if not controlled. As humans are social creatures, it makes sense that we need others in our lives. Disorders such as depression, anxiety, and borderline personality disorder can make us think the opposite - that we should be alone.

If we continue to think this way, then our interpersonal effectiveness skills won't have a chance to work. The more effort you put in and the more committed you are to making changes in your life, the better your relationships will be. It can be really difficult to develop interpersonal effectiveness skills on your own, but classes can help tremendously. Through DBT classes, you can learn much about yourself, practice your communication skills, and make new friends along the way.

Chapter Five: Emotion Regulation Skills

Emotion regulation is the ability to balance your emotions effectively within different situations and around different people. People who suffer from borderline personality disorder or other mood disorders struggle with managing their emotions. Throughout childhood development, most kids learn how to regulate their emotions as a result of being around role models and having positive influences. However, not everyone learns this important skill; for example, people who have lived through difficult trauma or who were not taught how to self-regulate may struggle with it as adults. Emotion regulation is the ability to manage, cope with, and understand every emotion that passes through us. So, if we are feeling distressed, someone who knows how to self-regulate could define that emotion and figure out a way to bring themselves to a better emotional state. A person without these self-regulation skills, however, won't be able to effectively change their mood, and might react in an impulsive or inappropriate way.

Emotional dysregulation is common in people who suffer from eating disorders, and BPD. Simply put, it is the inability to regulate your emotions that results in behavior disorders and impulsive decision making. Emotional dysregulation can also be found in people that have narcissistic personalities and other distinct personality disorders. They can be manipulative, controlling, and aggressive, and generally like to cause conflict. Because these people are misunderstood and cannot regulate emotions properly and effectively, it can cause them problems in their personal life, work life, and in relationships.

Symptoms of emotional dysregulation:

- Always wanting to control the behaviors of people, and the environments around them
- Blaming others and never taking responsibility
- Hanging onto anger and holding grudges
- Creating and anticipating conflict
- Feeling entitled
- Never seeming to have a rational point or a logical solution when in heated arguments
- A tendency to self-harm like cutting or developing an eating disorder

Some people just struggle with these symptoms from time to time and maybe only experience one or two of them. However, in 80% of cases, someone that suffers from a mood disorder will have two or more of these symptoms. The struggle with emotional dysregulation is that people who suffer from it constantly have a difficult time cooperating and socializing with people.

Here are some examples of ways through which emotion regulation is both learned, and implemented:

1. **Influential change in someone else.**

   If you are a parent, you will want to teach your child how to regulate their emotions. Every child has temper tantrums, and although they may make you angry or amused, you should fight the urge to yell or laugh. Instead, you need to regulate your own emotions and talk calmly about what they are doing, and suggest better ways they could react besides throwing a tantrum. This is called **extrinsic emotion regulation**.

2. **Influential change in yourself.**

   If you want to become more positive, you can begin by consciously challenging your negative thoughts and replacing them with positive ones. This is referred to as **intrinsic emotion regulation**. It is driven by our culture, our view or morals, and our perception of our environment.

3. **Changing your emotions**

   Changing the intensity, duration, and type of our emotions depending on the situation we are in is another example of what emotion regulation is. For example, we may feel anxious in a social setting; however, no one else will notice or know about it. We can also change how long our emotions will linger for. For example, you might avoid feeling anxious over the stress in your life by distracting your mind with other things. Another example of changing the type of emotion we are experiencing is when we do something embarrassing like tripping over. Instead of feeling ashamed, you could choose to just laugh it off.

4. **Unconscious regulation**

   This kind of regulation stems from changing your emotions without noticing. An example would be if you change the channel on the TV to stop yourself from becoming upset by what you were watching. You may not fully realize that you did it, but your subconscious kicked in and regulated your emotions for you.

Sometimes, the self-regulation of your emotions can overlap with each other. For example, you can use extrinsic regulation to calm your child, while actually, you are trying to calm your own anger or frustration in a healthy setting (intrinsic).

The third module in DBT is used to teach the individual how to manage their negative emotions and to increase their positive experiences. The goals of this module are:

- To understand other's emotions
- Reduce vulnerability regarding emotions
- Decrease the suffering associated with emotions

The idea behind the treatment and training is to help the individual understand that negative emotions are not to be labeled as "bad" and that they don't need to be rejected or avoided. The goal is to deal with your emotions individually and understand where they are coming from, so that you can let them go rather than being controlled by them. There is a cycle that people with extreme sensitivity to emotions go through. First, they undergo an event that triggers a negative thought. These negative thoughts turn into unwanted emotional responses, which then lead to destructive and impulsive behaviors.

What is Self-Regulation?

Self-regulation is something we do subconsciously without putting much thought into it. We may hear these questions from our children (or remember asking when we were children): "Why can't we eat cake for breakfast"? or "Why do adults get to do whatever they want"? This is a prime example of what self-regulation is. Sure, we can do whatever we want as adults. We can skip work or eat cake for breakfast if we want. However, we don't because we have self-regulation skills.

The ability to gain or regain control over a behavior or life situations is what we refer to as self-regulation. When psychologists use the term self-regulation, there are two types:

1. Behavioral
2. Emotional

What is Behavioral Self-Regulation?

Behavioral self-regulation is defined as being able to feel one way but then acting differently than how we feel. For example, it's like when we wake up and don't want to go to work. Then we remember our goals (get a promotion, create a legacy, or be a good role model) or our needs (food, shelter, money, etc.) and we get up and continue to go to work. This is behavioral self-regulation.

What is Emotional Self-Regulation?

This term relates more to taking control of your emotions. You display effective emotional self-regulation when you talk yourself down from an anxious mood or calm yourself down when you are angry. The result would be that you went from a negative emotional state to a more positive one on your own.

Essential Emotion-Regulation Coping Skills

Emotion regulation is essential because its sole purpose is to identify, manage, and respond to how you are internally feeling. This allows you to put your emotions to use when you need to act in a particular circumstance. Depending on the situation, emotional regulation typically consists of you calming your emotions or tapping into them. When you practice mindfulness, you can become more in tune with your feelings and with your body. When you are mindful of your emotions, you can watch them go from overwhelming, paralyzing, and confusing, to calm, relaxed, and focused.

One thing to take note of is that emotions are not "good" nor are they "bad." Emotions, like thoughts, are just emotions; that's all they are, and we don't need to put any emphasis on labeling them. The reason most people label emotions as good or bad is due to the feeling they get from experiencing them. So, if we feel anxious, we may develop symptoms of constant sweating, trembling, and increased heart rate. However, if we look at the emotion itself, it's just anxiety, and like thoughts or anything else in life, this emotion will come, and then it will go. Just be mindful of the experience. There is no need to try to change it, give in to the symptoms our feelings have created, or give ourselves judgment based on our emotions.

If you are a person who experiences emotion dysregulation, you may want to try out the following coping strategies:

1. **Understand your emotions**

    All too often we act too quickly on our emotions because we are fearful of them, or we give in to the desire to act impulsively Try taking a step back and looking at your emotions as if they belonged to someone else; look at them from a third person point of view. Give yourself time to name the emotion and notice what symptoms you are feeling from it. Take a step away from yourself for just a moment and watch what your emotion is doing. This may sound easier said than done. Be truthful with yourself at the moment your emotion is taking place. How well have you been able to manage or "regulate" this specific emotion? Would your life be different if every time you felt an overwhelming emotion, you took a step back and just watched it instead? What if you became mindful of it?

2. **Allow exposure to your emotions**

   Negative emotions are like a bully, or a bored little brother or sister. They will poke you just because they are bored, and the more you avoid them or ignore them, the more annoying or frustrating they become. The trick to chasing away the bully or creating boundaries with your siblings is that, much like emotions, you have to acknowledge them. Say, "I know you are here, you are overwhelming me, and I need some space." By doing this, you acknowledge your emotions but don't give in to them by "poking" back. You've created a secure boundary and asked for what you need. Negative emotions won't just go away when you ask them to, but over time you will learn to sit patiently with your emotions without judging them as good or bad.

3. **Use counterconditioning strategies**

   The idea behind this is that your original response to what you are feeling needs to be replaced with a new response. One technique that falls under counterconditioning is called "systematic desensitization." This can be taught to you by a DBT specialist and involves a range of relaxation methods that can help you to remain calm when experiencing a strong emotion.

4. **Increase positivity**

    Have you ever heard the saying, "You are what you eat" or "You are what you think"? Maybe you even thought, "I am what I do." This way of thinking can actually make you experience more negative emotions, distressing thoughts, and impulsive behaviors. As capable as you might be of telling yourself that you aren't good enough, you are just as capable of telling yourself that you are good enough and that your self-worth is important. Intentionally create positive space in your mind and choose gratitude over hate. Choose to forgive others, rather than hold grudges or resentment. Try the following activities if you're struggling to maintain positive self-talk:

    a. Talk it out with a loved one
    b. Take a soothing bubble bath
    c. Go for a nature walk or hike
    d. Listen to calming music
    e. Write in a journal

5. **Increase the quality of your coping skills**

    Just like anything you do that is new, you need to practice at it for a while to become proficient. Learning to regulate your emotions can be a difficult task;

however, the more you practice, the better at it you will be until it becomes second nature. When you learn how to manage, control, and understand your emotions, they will no longer take control of your life. As you practice regulating your emotions, you will become better at noticing when they first arise and being able to instantly switch to being mindful of your emotions rather than acting on them. You will start to notice your triggers, and feel more prepared to deal with overwhelming situations and emotions.

Skills Used in DBT Therapy for Emotion Regulation

The following skills taught in DBT therapy help an individual reduce vulnerability, increase resilience, and improve overall mental health. In DBT, distress tolerance skills will help you cope with your emotions, and emotion regulation exercises will help prevent overwhelming emotions from occurring. The module includes understanding our emotions, ABC PLEASE, and opposite action.

Understanding Our Emotions

Every emotion we experience plays an important role in why we are feeling the way we are. The feelings we experience tell us when a situation is frightening, and we shouldn't continue, or if a situation is friendly, and we should continue. This is often referred to as the "gut feeling." Have you ever walked up to someone, but then felt anxious out of nowhere? So, you stayed on your guard, and were cautious the whole interaction. Our instincts are not always right, but it is a good idea to listen to them most of the time. Also, our emotions let people know how we are feeling nonverbally through our body language.

Emotions are an important part of our lives, because they can make us anxious when we need to be, empathetic when appropriate, and friendly when we want or need something. We need our emotions to sympathize and cheer others up, or to defend ourselves when we are in a difficult situation.

Understanding your emotions involves you being mindful of your emotions and then considering where they are coming from and why. The emotion may be trying to tell you something is off. Then, you can decide whether you should pay attention to this emotion, or instead, let it go.

ABC PLEASE

The ABC PLEASE skill helps us to decrease our vulnerability to our emotions, or rather, the impact our emotions have on us.

1. **A - Accumulating positive experiences**

    Most negative experiences won't seem as harmful or damaging when we focus on our long-term goals. By focusing on the bigger picture, these negative experiences can be viewed as learning lessons, or speedbumps, rather than anything too serious. To complete our long-term goals, we need to actively involve ourselves in a variety of positive activities while working toward them.

2. **B - Build mastery**

    This skill teaches us to develop our abilities. It helps us to focus on our talents and how we can improve or develop them. If you are good at writing, then DBT encourages you to work on your writing, reading, and editing skills. If you are talented at drawing or hearing tones when listening to music, DBT helps you improve these skills further so that you can feel a sense of accomplishment and success on a daily basis. As we further develop the skills that we are already good at, we become more confident. With confidence comes the willingness to try new things and to become good at them too. The idea here is to show you that our emotions are just emotions, and that there is more to life than just focusing on how you feel.

3. **C - Cope ahead**

To cope ahead means to prepare for the negative situation before it happens. Through the exercises of DBT, you will learn what triggers you, and then through coping ahead, you can learn how to manage your emotions before the trigger occurs.

PLEASE

The PLEASE skills are designed to help us take care of ourselves and our well-being. Our physical health, what we eat, our sleeping schedule, and daily routine, all play a part in our mental health. It's when we are sick, drained, or unhealthy that we experience negative emotions the most. So, by caring for ourselves we increase the chance of having more positive experiences. PLEASE means:

- PL = Treating Physical illness

- E = Balanced Eating
- A = Avoid mood-altering drugs and alcohol
- S = Balanced Sleep
- E = Exercise

Opposite Action

Opposite action has to do with controlling your emotions when they don't fit the scenario. Every emotion comes with an urge or behavior, but that doesn't mean you have to give in to that urge. Every time you are experiencing an emotion, take a step back. Figure out which urge or action you associate with that emotion. For example, anxiety can come with the urge to run or fight back. If you feel happy, or excited, you might feel the urge to jump, or smile.

The urges that you feel when you have emotions are intended to protect you; however, when your behaviors are abnormal, this may not always be the case. For example, if you need to speak in front of a large group but feel anxious and your anxiety makes you want to run, the behavior behind the emotion doesn't fit. So, the purpose of opposite actions means that when your behavior doesn't fit your emotion, you will have to intentionally train yourself to do the opposite of your urge. For example, if all you want to do is isolate yourself when you feel depressed, fight against this urge and seek out interaction with a friend. People who suffer from mood disorders such as anxiety and BPD may find this technique especially helpful because it teaches them to rewire their brain to do the opposite of what their emotions suggest. Over time, your brain will begin to associate those emotions with the more appropriate behaviors you implemented.

DBT emotion-regulation for opposite actions works best if it is developed alongside other skills. This means that not only do you train your behaviors to be the opposite of your emotions, but your thoughts and words should become the opposite of your emotions as well.

Every time you practice a skill taken from DBT, you are rewiring your brain to think, act, and perceive differently. Over time you will feel better and experience fewer impulses. DBT's purpose is to help maintain positive attitudes, keep healthy relationships, reduce negative feelings, and decrease the impact that negative thoughts and feelings have on us. Emotion regulation skills teach us that by taking care of ourselves, defining our emotions, and acting opposite to our urges we can develop real control over our feelings and how we respond to them.

Chapter Summary

Emotion regulation is not just about "regulating" your emotions; it is also about learning to take care of yourself after you complete this module. It's about developing the life skills that many people never get to learn. Emotion regulation skills aim to help you understand yourself better, while also gaining an understanding of how others process their emotions. Actively working on your emotional intelligence while also undergoing a treatment course of DBT will allow you to experience the full benefits of what this module has to teach you.

Chapter Six: DBT and Mental Illnesses

Dialectical behavior therapy is a type of therapy that revolves around being mindful of our emotions, how to regulate them, cope with them, and use them to become better communicators. It teaches us important skills like how to behave in public and personal environments, how to get what you want without your emotions taking complete control of you, and how to deal with extreme emotions when we feel we cannot handle them. It is especially effective in overcoming or managing borderline personality disorder, addictions, and eating disorders. DBT is closely related to, and stems from, cognitive behavior therapy (CBT) which helps people to cope with anxiety, PTSD, and depression. However, DBT has been shown to provide people with the right tools and skills to manage these issues as well, perhaps even more effectively than CBT.

In this chapter, we will discuss a variety of disorders, and how CBT and DBT can work together to help people deal with and manage these mood disorders. We will also explain why DBT is often the better treatment, and why you should take the time to sit with a professional and work through your mental health issues using the framework of DBT. In the first chapter, we mentioned that DBT can help with borderline personality disorder, and also explained some of the differences between cognitive and dialectical behavior therapies. In this chapter we'll take it a step further and have a closer look at how DBT can help with other mood disorders as well.

Anxiety Disorder

Anxiety can vary greatly from person to person, and there are multiple types of anxiety that can result in the diagnosis of a disorder. Anxiety disorder also often exhibits a bunch of symptoms that are more commonly associated with BPD, or depression. Anxiety is broadly defined as a feeling of worry, nervousness, or unease about something with an uncertain outcome. Like most mood disorders, the cause of anxiety often stems from childhood trauma, genetics, or a combination of the two. It usually starts to appear in adolescence, and if not properly treated can lead to more mental health issues such as schizophrenia, dissociative disorder, depression, and psychosis. Luckily, DBT can be very helpful in teaching a person methods of managing and eventually overcome their anxiety.

DBT and Anxiety

DBT teaches the skills needed to manage anxiety symptoms in four distinct sections - core mindfulness, distress tolerance, emotional regulation, and interpersonal effectiveness. In each module, there are simple techniques that can be learned to help cope with, and understand, the feelings of anxiety.

Let's take a walk through of some skills that DBT teaches for managing anxiety:

Core Mindfulness

As a refresher, mindfulness practices go back thousands of years with religions such as Buddhism, Hinduism, Islam, Judaism, and Christianity. The main focus of mindfulness is to be mindful of your surroundings, and the way you are feeling. It's to breathe peacefully and develop a sense of calmness without doing anything other than focusing on being in that exact moment.

The module for this exercise divides your mind into three parts, looking at it as the "wise mind," the "emotional mind," and the "reasonable mind." The idea of managing your anxiety through these three "minds" is that you blend and balance the messages coming from the emotional and reasonable mind to obtain a wise mind. Basically, the idea is to balance two opposites (reason and emotion) and merge them into one solution (the wise mind).

Distress Tolerance

With anxiety, we tend to want to control everything in an attempt to not have an anxiety or panic attack. Distress tolerance teaches us ways to cope with not having total control and helps us to accept a given situation without panicking. Anxiety can give us overwhelming feelings of distress due to our heightened and over-the-top emotions. So, the best way to cope with this is to change our biology.

There is this neat thing called "the dive reflex." It is a built-in hack that actually works to calm us down when we are stressed. The dive reflex occurs when you splash water on your face, causing your body to relax automatically. This is because when we dive, we instinctively want to save our breath, and it subconsciously makes us relax. So, when you feel distressed, overwhelmed, anxious, or panicked, try splashing cold water on your face to calm down.

Emotional-Regulation

Do you find that you often feel worried or frightened by things that are not actually harmful? Do you ever experience panic attacks? These emotional responses to events in life are meant to protect us from danger, but in a person with anxiety, they often occur at times when they're totally unnecessary. Emotional regulation teaches you to respond to these emotions and create preventative measures so that you can stop them from becoming too overwhelming.

Through the opposite action technique, you can learn how to redirect your emotions from wanting to run based on feelings of anxiety, to sitting with and coping with your emotions. Opposite actions help you understand when you should act in the opposite manner to what your emotion is suggesting. For example, let's imagine you are about to make a speech in front on a large audience. You will likely experience anxiety, and your emotions will tell you to run away and hide. This is a perfect time to implement opposite action. In that situation, you need to face your fear, and give the speech. This has the effect of lessening your anxiety the next time you find yourself having to give a speech, whereas had you listened to your emotions and ran away, your anxiety would only worsen in the future.

Using your mindfulness skills, you can really tap into your emotions and what you are feeling throughout your body to figure out what you should do about those feelings. Take a few deep breaths and splash cold water on your face. Then, by acting the opposite to your urges, you will feel a sense of accomplishment after you have fully calmed down. After this process is repeated enough times, most people will notice their anxiety begins to decrease and they gain a better control over their emotional responses.

Interpersonal Effectiveness

If you feel like people take advantage of you because you have a hard time saying no, this can cause you distress and anxiety. You may feel overworked or overwhelmed with obligations that you don't actually want. If you also experience that people don't listen to you, or that you are often picked on or victimized by others, interpersonal effectiveness will likely benefit you.

In DBT, you learn the DEAR MAN technique which is designed to make it easier for you to assert yourself and negotiate effectively. DEAR is expanded into describe, express, assert, reinforce. MAN is expanded into mindfulness, appearing confident, and negotiating. The DEAR section requires that you act upon the skills in sequential order. For the MAN part, you can apply these skills in any order.

In short, the purpose of DEAR MAN is to state what you want, express your needs effectively, assert what you are asking for respectively, and then finish with reinforcement. The MAN part of the technique is about your attitude. You need to have good posture, speak confidently, and be mindful of your emotions at the moment in which you're speaking. If you don't get the answer you want right away, MAN teaches you how to negotiate effectively to get what you want without pushing your luck.

Eating Disorders

Eating disorders are diagnosed based on someone's eating patterns, moods, and other behaviors. They are characterized by abnormal eating habits such as starving oneself, vomiting after every meal, or binge eating. They usually coexist with anxiety disorders, substance abuse, or depression. The outward reason why someone develops an eating disorder appears to be that they either have an irrational fear of becoming overweight, or they already see themselves as too heavy or too skinny. However, internally, eating disorders are more focused on a need for control. Manipulating weight or body shape is merely the outward expression of that. The three main eating disorders are anorexia nervosa, bulimia nervosa, and binge-eating disorder.

Anorexia Nervosa

This type of eating disorder involves a person starving themselves in an attempt to lose weight because they have an obsessive fear of gaining weight or having any body fat. People suffering from anorexia nervosa see themselves as different than they actually look. Anorexia when it reaches extreme levels can lead to brain damage, multi-organ failure, bone loss, heart damage, and infertility. In some cases, anorexia can be fatal.

Bulimia Nervosa

Bulimia is a disorder where after eating, a person then attempts to compensate for the food they ate through forceful vomiting, excessive use of laxatives, extreme exercise, or future restriction of food. These people fear weight gain and are extremely unsatisfied with the way they look. Episodes of vomiting are typically done in secret, and they may feel ashamed, guilty, or embarrassed afterward. The damaging effects of bulimia are extreme dehydration, heart problems, and gastrointestinal problems resulting from an electrolyte imbalance.

Binge Eating Disorder

Binge eating disorder, or BED, can lead to cardiovascular disease and obesity, which may or may not cause other mental health problems. These people cannot control the amount they eat and become obsessed with food. They may experience feelings of guilt, embarrassment, and distress due to their body image. Some people affected by bulimia also binge eat before making themselves vomit, but they are different to those who just suffer from BED. Binge eating is different from bulimia because unlike bulimia, binge eating does not create disruptive behaviors such as purging, fasting, disposal, and excessive exercise. Binge eating is often used as a coping mechanism for people to deal with their emotions, and as such, BED often coexists with other mental health disorders such as anxiety, and depression.

Although CBT has been proven to help people with eating disorders, it is not the only therapy that can work. DBT can also assist someone suffering from an eating disorder because it teaches them how to express their emotions in a healthy way, rather than through their eating habits. Someone with binge eating disorder, for example, may feel stressed by events in their life and turn to food to deal with these negative feelings. DBT can teach them to accept, understand, and manage the stress they are experiencing in healthy ways, rather than through excessive eating.

DBT teaches mindfulness techniques that help people to be in the moment with their urges. With practice, they will learn that their urges pass if they acknowledge them but don't pay attention or give in to them. Distress tolerance is used for helping the patient cope with their emotions or feelings relating to their body image and food. Emotion regulation will prevent unhelpful emotions from controlling the individual. Finally, interpersonal effectiveness teaches strategies to overcome the challenges associated with saying no, especially to themselves.

Urges won't be as hard to control, behaviors will become healthy, and emotions won't feel so intense or unmanageable when DBT is used effectively. Also, with the many ways someone can experience DBT – group settings, office settings, or the comfort of home over the phone – the individual won't feel as vulnerable as when implementing other therapies such as CBT. Unlike CBT, dialectical behavior therapy gives you skills and resources you can take home with you. This way, when the individual is struggling on their own, they have the tools required help them with their specific issue.

PTSD

Post-traumatic stress disorder, or PTSD, is a type of anxiety disorder that's triggered by past trauma, and often involves experiencing flashbacks. Symptoms include waking from nightmares of the event, which results in a panic attack, and experiencing intrusive thoughts associated with the event. Anything can set off a PTSD panic attack, from a certain smell to a certain image, or even a particular person. This is because anything associated with the traumatic event can trigger a disturbing memory, or a distressing emotion.

An individual with PTSD may try to avoid people, places, or things in order to stop the memory from entering their mind. In some instances, they may view themselves as deserving of the negative feelings associated with the event. They may also feel useless in present circumstances or hopeless at ever having a bright and successful future. Hobbies and interests won't feel as interesting anymore, and they may develop a deep depression or extreme anxiety as a side effect of their PTSD. Intimate relationships may be hard to maintain due to their experiences, friendships may be short, and careers can be impacted due to the emotional baggage the individual carries around with them.

The changes in emotional and physical behavior may include being easily frightened, feeling tense or on edge most of the time, and implementing self-destructive behavior as a way to cope. Sleeping habits may be greatly affected due to constant nightmares, concentration may be difficult due to the lack of sleep, and emotions may be hard to control.

How DBT Can Help

DBT helps people with personality disorders, anxiety disorders, eating disorders, substance abuse, and addiction problems. What they all have in common are problems with regulating their emotions and being impulsive. Most people who suffer from PTSD are at risk for suicide, as many people develop self-harming behaviors as a coping mechanism. When their body becomes numb to the pain that they are inflicting on themselves, suicide is the next step that a lot of these people take. DBT can help save a life by teaching the individual with PTSD healthy avoidance techniques, mindfulness grounding strategies, relationship building, and emotional regulation methods to prevent these flashbacks or memories from controlling their life.

Mindfulness

Mindfulness can create a distance between the past event and the current moment, which can make a person with PTSD feel much better. As mindfulness teaches things like grounding and being in the present moment. When the victim is flooded with memories and nightmares, mindfulness will help the person bring themselves back to the present moment. It can help the individual be in the moment with their friends, and relationships, as well as help them focus on their careers.

Mindfulness can teach awareness, nonjudgmental observation, and being in the present moment. Through awareness techniques, it will teach the individual to experience a greater awareness of their surroundings and how they are feeling at any given moment in time. Mindfulness is about teaching the individual how to respond to the here and now rather, than being focused back in the past. It helps the victim notice their sensations (thoughts and feelings) and their surroundings (sights and sounds) nonjudgmentally and without fear.

Distress Tolerance

Distress tolerance teaches how to survive an emotional disturbance without making it worse. It also gives you the skills and knowledge of how to take back control of your life. The frightening emotions an individual with PTSD can feel are shame, guilt, extreme anxiety, and sadness. Those with PTSD may experience other side effects like self-harm, binge eating, no eating, substance abuse, or other disruptive impulsive behaviors.

Distress tolerance helps you to prepare and cope with your extreme emotions and be able to effectively replace these emotions with positivity. A treatment called interoceptive exposure is taught within this DBT module, and it helps with your ability to withstand the symptoms brought about by your emotions.

Distraction is one of the techniques you learn in the distress tolerance module, and some distraction techniques are as follows:

- Getting active - Do something you enjoy like going for a walk, reading a book, or engaging in a hobby.

- Contributing - Contributing is about doing something for others. Get outside your comfort zone and help someone today. Is there a neighbor that needs help around the house? Is there a friend that is moving and needs help packing? Maybe you're going for a walk and see someone needs help to unload their groceries. No matter how big your contribution, helping others is a great way to improve the emotions you experience.

- Triggering opposite emotions - If you are feeling sad, do the opposite and smile. If you are feeling angry, watch or do something that makes you want to laugh. Most of the time, you will feel better.

- Think big - The idea of this exercise is to fill your brain with bigger things than your distressing feelings so that there is no room for your distress to take over. Think about every detail of how you would re-organize your home, or if you are in public, look at a stranger and imagine a fake life that you think would suit them. Try anything to distract your mind from being upset.

- Self-soothe - This technique uses skills developed from mindfulness. Use all six of your senses, including movement (which DBT considers to be a sense). Reward yourself with something you have been wanting for a while. Maybe it is a watch or piece of jewelry you've been wanting. Or it could be something simple like treating yourself to ice cream. When you do this, think about how you would soothe someone in your current situation. Try treating yourself the same way.

- Putting your body in charge - The idea behind this exercise is that in response to what your body does, your mind and emotions will react appropriately. So, get exercising, lift some weights, run up and down the stairs, or go for a brisk walk. Your mind will respond to the exercise seesion with positive emotions, and a release of endorphins.

Emotion regulation

Having PTSD can be just as damaging as any other mental health disorder. You may be completely fine at one moment, laughing with your friends, and then you hear ambulance sirens or see something that triggers you into a complete panic attack. This can leave you wanting to run, or cry, or even get angry. Emotion regulation provides you with the tools needed to counteract these urges and provide relief to your emotions.

One of the ways to regain control of your PTSD symptoms through DBT emotion regulation is to increase your heart rate variability (HRV). The higher your HRV, the more your system is relaxed and adaptable; the lower your HRV is, the less relaxed and adaptable you become. This affects the vagus nerve function, which is a cranial nerve that connects your brain to your internal organs in your chest, abdomen, and pelvis. In short, the healthier your vagus nerve system is, the more regulated your emotions are.

Some ways you can keep your HRV high and you vagus nerve happy are:

- Meditation - Focus on your breath for five minutes.

- Breathwork - Inhale through your nose, and exhale through pursed lips. The goal is to get under six breaths per minute.

- Cardio - this includes running, walking, or anything similar.

By doing these exercises, your system will begin to feel safer and calmer. When your system feels better, emotion regulation becomes easy to practice. Another way to reclaim your control is to focus on being non-judgmental. When you force yourself into a state of non-evaluation, your nervous system finds it difficult to fire false alarms and defense mechanisms. Some ways to practice non-judgment are as follows:

- Self-compassion - Treating yourself with kindness in the face of perceived danger puts your brain into a safe state.

- Release judgment - If you are negative with yourself and other people, your brain is always in a defense mode. By being aware of these negative judgments, you can train your brain into a state of safety by letting go of previously conceived notions of yourself and others.

- Interoception - You learn this technique in almost every module. Interoception is the ability to be aware of what's happening in your body. Some practices that teach this include yoga, mindfulness, and concentration.

Depression

Clinical depression is a mood disorder caused by a variety of factors including personality, stress, genetics, and brain chemistry. Depression isn't simply when you feel unhappy or constant sadness. Depression is when you cannot fight distressing emotions such as extreme unhappiness, numbness, and feelings of hopelessness or uselessness.

Some forms of depression include:

- **Seasonal Affective disorder (SAD):** This type of depression is just as it sounds: seasonal. This is when people become depressed or have depressive symptoms through fall and winter, which are often the rainy seasons.

- **Postpartum Depression**: This happens after childbirth when mothers experience the side effects of giving birth, the newness of their child, and other dramatic changes in their lives.

- **Depression with psychosis**: When depression becomes too extreme, psychosis can occur, which then makes the person loses touch with what's real and what's not. It is as if everything feels like a dream, and the person can experience delusions and hallucinations.

- **Dysthymia**: This disorder is when a person experiences a chronically low mood all the time, but it's not quite as extreme as depression. However, depression can set in periodically with moderate symptoms.

The symptoms of depression are as follows:
- Changes in weight and appetite
- Sleep disturbances
- Loss of interest in things you used to love
- Withdrawal from people and close bonds
- Tiredness or irritation and feeling sluggish or slow
- Difficult time concentrating
- Mood changes or cry easily and often
- Thoughts of suicide and self-harm

- Psychosis

Dialectical behavior therapy can help with depression because it encourages self-acceptance and change. It is geared toward skills that help you to validate yourself and others, as well as tolerate the extreme emotions you experience. According to the National Alliance on Mental Illness (NAMI), DBT for depression will help to:

- Improve motivation through positive reinforcement and encouragement to adjust your inhibitions
- Decrease destructive behaviors
- Help regulate and understand your emotions
- Promote understanding of the actions you do based on how you are feeling
- Use preventative measures to avoid experiencing extreme depressive symptoms

The goal of treating depression through dialectical behavior therapy is to teach the individual crucial skills to help cope with daily life activities.

Mindfulness

In the DBT module of core mindfulness, you learn to be totally aware of the symptoms you experience while in a depressive state. This can help you to take notice of your thoughts nonjudgmentally. This is of benefit because it allows you to separate yourself from your depression and gain a full understanding of how your thoughts are affecting your behavior. It should leave you less stressed and more relaxed when you come back from your mindfulness meditation. Once you've become proficient at mindfulness meditation, you can practice mindfulness throughout the day when doing things like washing dishes or reading a book.

Mindfulness can help depression in adults by giving the patient the skills needed to pay attention what is going on inside them. They then begin notice their unhealthy thought patterns, the feelings stemming from these thoughts, the sensations in their body, and their dangerous impulses. Mindfulness also helps the patient bring their focus to what's going on around them such as what they see, hear, smell, feel, and taste.

With regular practice of mindfulness for depression, you can see benefits such as:

- Increased emotion regulation ability

- Decreased difficulties in focusing while learning helpful ways to concentrate

- Decreased likelihood of having extreme mood changes like irritability to sadness to anger

- Better control of the impulsive behavior urges

- Increased immunity

Interpersonal Effectiveness

Interpersonal effectiveness skills work just the same as a short-term treatment with antidepressant medication. These skills were developed to help adults, children, and adolescents treat their depression. The short-term goals for this therapy are to decrease depressive symptoms and improve social adjustment. The long-term goal is to provide people with the ability to make their own adjustments without the help of a therapist. When they are fully capable of doing this on their own, depressive symptoms will seem increasingly distant or unnoticeable.

The three components of interpersonal effectiveness help a depressed individual with:

- Symptom formation
- Social functioning
- Personality issues

The interpersonal effectiveness skills you learn through this module of DBT will help you become more aware of how you are feeling when socializing. Over time, you may find that it becomes easier to talk to people and be sociable when you need to be. Through distress tolerance and emotion regulation, you will learn strategies to counteract negative thoughts when they arise. And with mindfulness, you will be able to become conscious of your negative thinking patterns as soon as they occur, and then make the necessary changes to stop them in their tracks.

Distress Tolerance

People who don't understand depression don't know the overwhelming feelings of misery that depression can cause on a daily basis. Those who suffer from depression can understand what it feels like to feel alienated from the world. Distress tolerance helps the individual understand why these emotions happen and implement healthy ways of coping with these feelings. When someone experiences depression, they may feel ashamed or embarrassed about their disorder, so they isolate themselves in an attempt to hide their suffering. These people often put on a brave face and pretend as though everything is okay. If the depression is not dealt with, it can worsen and result in self-harm, or suicide.

The problem with pretending that everything is okay, is that people begin to think they can manage their depression on their own, simply by avoiding or eliminating their thoughts and feelings as quickly as possible. In distress tolerance, they will learn that ignoring their emotions and pushing thoughts away does not help. Instead, undergoing the distress tolerance module can teach ways to deal with and recognize these strong emotions by doing the opposite: Paying attention to them and labeling them while practicing mindfulness to let them go.

What can happen with depression is that family and friends become confused because they don't see the underlying cause; they only see the behaviors surrounding the disorder that push them away. This can leave the depressed individual physically lonely which results in feeling mentally and emotionally alone as well. Distress tolerance can teach an individual how to cope with their emotions and react differently to their urges by acting the opposite to what they feel, leaving them in a state where they don't push people away and can maintain and balance healthy relationships.

After practicing distress tolerance, you must still develop self-care strategies, which distress tolerance also helps with. You will learn how to re-energize and motivate yourself to continue getting up each day and pushing forward, despite feeling down and vulnerable.

Substance Use and Addictions

Substance use is when people use substances such as stimulants (cocaine and speed), depressants (alcohol and Valium), opiates (morphine and heroin), hallucinogens (LSD and mushrooms), or any other drugs. Addiction occurs when the person becomes tolerant of the substance and continues to chase the "high" or euphoric feeling they experienced the first time they took it. An addiction is when someone becomes dependent on the substance to function in an everyday setting.

There are two types of dependencies:

- **Physical Dependence** - This is when someone has become immune or tolerant to a substance, and when they suddenly stop taking it, they feel negative symptoms called withdrawals.
- **Psychological Dependence** - Psychological dependence is when the person experiences the need for the substance mentally; they strongly believe that without it they won't be able to function properly.

Withdrawals happen when a person stops taking a substance and experiences physical and mental symptoms as a result of no longer taking the drug. Many people smoke, drink, and do drugs to escape from underlying problems, the demands of life, and the overwhelming emotions they experience on a day to day basis. However, taking drugs to escape these things is not a permanent or healthy solution.

Withdrawal symptoms can include:

- Tension
- Panic attacks
- Tremors
- Difficulty focusing
- Irritability
- Short temper
- Sleep disturbance
- Nausea and vomiting
- Fast or slow heart rate
- Headache
- Cold and hot chills

These symptoms of withdrawal are just scratching the surface of what many people experience when abstaining from a drug they have taken regularly. When withdrawing, extreme emotions often take place in the mind that can cause an individual to do almost anything to chase the high once again.

There are different stages of substance use:

- **Non-use** - not using anything at all.

- **Experimental use** - The first time someone tries a drug or drink is often because they are curious about the effects. They may try it to fit in or they might believe that no addiction will result from it.

- **Social use** - This is when a person takes drugs, drinks alcohol, or smokes pot and cigarettes when around others that do it. The substances are also used as a "party favor," which set the group up to have a fun evening.

- **Regular use** - Regular use of substances is when an individual makes the drugs a habitual routine and do them every day. They don't think much about it and have created a routine around their substance use. For example, they may use drugs at specific times such as after they eat, when they wake up, before they go to bed, etc.

- **Problematic use** - This stage in the process of substance use means that you have passed the addictive stage and now you will go to great lengths to get what you need, no matter what. This stage can ruin yours and others' lives because all you can think about is the drug, the high, the fix that you get from the substance. Without it, life becomes complicated, and everything becomes heightened.

There are many signs that a person may be using some type of addictive substance.

Behavioral Signs:

- Change in attitude or personality for no clear reason
- Change in social interactions, friends, or new hangouts
- Avoids people they used to socialize with; the company they keep have the same habit
- Drop in performance at work, or grades in school
- Forgetful
- Uninterested in activities or events that they used to partake in
- Oversensitivity or becoming resentful
- Secretive, suspicious, and always wanting privacy
- Always needing money

Physical Signs

- Change in eating habits and appetite; weight gain or weight loss
- Sleep disturbance, fatigue, and awake at weird hours

- Watery, red, or puffy eyes; pupils seem large or small; blank stare
- Shaky
- Extremely talkative or suddenly quiet (different from normal behavior)
- Runny nose or cough
- Nausea, vomiting, and sweating
- Abnormal heartbeat

People who suffer from addiction need motivation and willpower to recover; however, recovery takes a lot more than these two things to completely rid themselves of their habit. Addiction is not just exclusive to drugs and alcohol; someone can be addicted to sexual activity, pornography, gambling, the internet, and technology.

The skills learned in DBT teach people to say no to the addictive habit. This ability to say no is developed through a combination of mindfulness, interpersonal skills, emotion regulation, and distress tolerance. Mindfulness allows them to notice their urges and respond logically rather than just give in to their addictions. Distress tolerance teaches individuals how to ride out their urges and manage their cravings. After the cravings subside, many heightened emotions may be present which is where emotion regulation comes in. DBT covers all aspects of addiction recovery to bring an individual to a place of self-care, confidence, and emotional stability.

When someone chooses to try DBT therapy for their addictive problems and substance use, they may be unsure of what to expect. There are four stages for the client to complete during the treatment. The main goals are as follows:

Stage One: Transitioning from losing control to being in complete control.

The individual will learn strategies to help them increase focus, improve healthy relationships, define what unhealthy relationships are, understand the distress they feel, and learn how to manage it. Often when someone has a substance use problem, they will become reckless and act upon their impulsive urges.

Stage Two: Transitioning from emotional instability to emotional stability.

As a coping mechanism, people will often shut their emotions down because they are too difficult to handle. This stage teaches people how to tap into their emotions and deal with them through positive engagement. The end goal of stage two is to let the individual embrace their feelings without relying on avoidance behaviors and escape routines.

Stage Three: Learning to live a normal life with normal problems.

This stage shows the individual that the problems they face now like suicidality, self-harm, and isolation are unhealthy and abnormal problems. It teaches the individual how to deal with normal problems such as career stress and how to manage a healthy long-lasting relationship. The treatment's main focus is to help the individual with life stressors such as life goals, conflicts, and mild mental health symptoms.

Stage Four: Transitioning from feeling incomplete and empty to feeling connected and whole.

The goal of the last stage of the treatment is to help the individual grow into who they are going to be, and to make changes for their future without the fear of having a relapse.

The point of DBT treatment is to allow a person to feel confident that they can implement change in their lives, to leave them feeling certain of their ability to overcome their addiction, and to help them live a healthy life without cravings and emotions taking power over them.

Chapter Summary

DBT is a proven method of helping many different types of people overcome various mental health problems. DBT treatment, although different for every person, has the potential to be life changing.

DBT is designed to help individuals develop skills in the following four groups: core mindfulness, distress tolerance, interpersonal effectiveness, and emotion regulation. In each module, every individual will learn tools designed to help them with their specific needs. The main reason why DBT is so highly recommended for treating mental health disorders is that it is not a "one size fits all" treatment like most others out there are.

Conclusion

Thank you for taking the time to read this book on dialectical behavior therapy.

By now, you should have a good understanding of the four modules of DBT, how DBT works, and what kinds of disorders it can effectively treat.

The next step is to consult with a professional DBT therapist and begin your own treatment if you think that it's something that would benefit you.

Once again, thank you for choosing this book. I hope you found it to be helpful, and I wish you the best of luck in your journey with DBT.

Resources

American Psychological Association (n.d.) Retrieved from https://www.apa.org/helpcenter/stress-kinds

Anxiety Relief Project – Managing Anxiety with Dialectical Behavior Therapy (2019, May 12) Retrieved from https://anxietyreliefproject.com/managing-anxiety-dialectical-behavior-therapy-dbt/

Bay Area DBT and Couples Counseling Center – Mindfulness in DBT: How this core skill can help you (2015, July 13) Retrieved from https://bayareadbtcc.com/mindfulness-in-dbt/

Borderline Personality Disorder Treatment – How DBT Helps in the Treatment of BPD (2014, October 09) Retrieved from https://www.borderlinepersonalitytreatment.com/how-dbt-helps-treat-bpd.html

CAMH -Depression (n.d.) Retrieved from https://www.camh.ca/en/health-info/mental-illness-and-addiction-index/depression

CAMH – Borderline Personality Disorder (BPD) (n.d.) Retrieved from https://www.camh.ca/en/health-info/mental-illness-and-addiction-index/borderline-personality-disorder

CAMH – Dialectical Behavior Therapy (n.d.) Retrieved from https://www.camh.ca/en/health-info/mental-illness-and-addiction-index/dialectical-behaviour-therapy

Clearview Treatment Programs – Dialectical Behavior Therapy for Depression Treatment (2019, April 26) Retrieved from https://www.clearviewtreatment.com/blog/dbt-depression-treatment/

Clearview Woman's Center | BPD Treatment Los Angeles – Emotion Dysregulation Treatment with DBT (n.d.) Retrieved from https://www.clearviewwomenscenter.com/emotion-dysregulation-therapy/

DBT Eating Disorder Treatment – How it works, Effectiveness Case Studies (n.d.) Retrieved from https://www.mirror-mirror.org/dbt-eating-disorder-treatment.htm

DBT Skills Group of NJ – The Four Skill Modules (n.d.) Retrieved from http://www.dbtskillsgroupnj.com/four-skill-modules/

DBT – New DBT Skills for Addictions (n.d.) Retrieved from http://dbtvancouver.com/new-dbt-skills-for-addictions/

DrugAbuse.com – Dialectical Behavior Therapy (DBT) for Addiction Treatment (2018, November 25) Retrieved from https://drugabuse.com/treatment-therapy/dialectical-behavior-therapy/

Eating Disorder Hope – Eating Disorders: Symptoms, Signs, Causes, and articles For treatment help (n.d.) Retrieved from https://www.eatingdisorderhope.com/information/eating-disorder

GoodTherapy.org – Emotion Regulation in Dialectical Behavior Therapy (2014, February 21) Retrieved from https://www.goodtherapy.org/blog/emotion-regulation-dialectical-behavior-therapy-dbt-0318135

Greater Good – Mindfulness Definition | What is Mindfulness? (n.d.) Retrieved from https://greatergood.berkeley.edu/topic/mindfulness/definition

Healthy Place – The Importance of Emotional Regulation in PTSD Recovery (n.d.) retrieved from https://www.healthyplace.com/blogs/traumaptsdblog/2013/02/the-importance-of-emotional-regulation-in-ptsd-recovery

HealthyPlace – Distress Tolerance in Important for Depression (n.d.) retrieved from https://www.healthyplace.com/blogs/copingwithdepression/2016/02/why-distress-tolerance-is-important-for-depression

Help Guide – Benefits of Mindfulness (2019, May 22) Retrieved from https://www.helpguide.org/harvard/benefits-of-mindfulness.htm/

Helpguide.org – Effective Communication (2019, May 31) Retrieved from https://www.helpguide.org/articles/relationships-communication/effective-communication.htm

Inbreathe – The History of Mindfulness (2016, June 13) Retrieved from https://inbreathe.com.au/the-history-of-mindfulness/

Kelty Mental Health – Substance Use Challenges (n.d.) Retrieved from https://keltymentalhealth.ca/substance-use-challenges

Mayo Clinic – Borderline personality disorder (2018, June 28) Retrieved from https://www.mayoclinic.org/diseases-conditions/borderline-personality-disorder/symptoms-causes/syc-20370237

Mayo Clinic – Post-traumatic Stress Disorder (2018, July 06) Retrieved from https://www.mayoclinic.org/diseases-conditions/post-traumatic-stress-disorder/symptoms-causes/syc-20355967

Medical News Today – Cognitive Behavioral Therapy: How does CBT work? (2018, September 25) Retrieved from https://www.medicalnewstoday.com/articles/296579.php

Mental Help Surviving Crisis Dialectical Behavior Therapy DBT Distress Tolerance Skills Comments – Surviving a Crisis: DBT distress tolerance (n.d.) Retrieved from https://www.mentalhelp.net/articles/surviving-a-crisis-dialectical-behavior-therapy-dbt-distress-tolerance-skills/

Mindful – What is mindfulness? (2019, January 08) Retrieved from https://www.mindful.org/what-is-mindfulness/

Mindfulness Muse – How to Apply Interpersonal Effectiveness Skills (2012, July 05) Retrieved from https://www.mindfulnessmuse.com/dialectical-behavior-therapy/how-to-apply-interpersonal-effectiveness-skills

Mindfulness Muse – How to Use Emotion Regulation Coping Skills (2012, July 06) retrieved from https://www.mindfulnessmuse.com/dialectical-behavior-therapy/how-to-use-emotion-regulation-coping-skills

Nick Wignall – How to Start Mindfulness Practice: A Quick Guide for Complete Beginners (2019, May 14) Retrieved from https://nickwignall.com/how-to-start-a-mindfulness-practice/

PSYBlog – Mindfulness Exercises: 8 That Fit Into Your Day (2016, October 16) Retrieved from https://www.spring.org.uk/2014/04/mindfulness-meditation-8-quick-exercises-that-easily-fit-into-your-day.php

Positive Psychology Program – What is Emotional Intelligence? +18 Ways To Improve It (2019, May 29) Retrieved from https://positivepsychologyprogram.com/emotional-intelligence-eq/

Positive Psychology Program – What is Self-Regulation? (2019, May 20) retrieved from https://positivepsychologyprogram.com/self-regulation/

Robert Street Clinic – How Interpersonal Effectiveness Skills Improve Social Interactions (2014, November 17) Retrieved from https://robertstclinic.co.nz/interpersonal-effectiveness-skills/

SUCCESS – 18 Traits of Emotionally Intelligent People (2019, May 18) Retrieved from https://www.success.com/18-signs-you-have-high-emotional-intelligence/

Skyland – 4 Differences between CBT and DBT and How to Tell Which is Right for You (n.d.) retrieved from https://www.skylandtrail.org/About/Blog/ctl/ArticleView/mid/567/articleId/6747/4-Differences-Between-CBT-and-DBT-and-How-to-Tell-Which-is-Right-for-You

Study.com (n.d.) Retrieved from https://study.com/academy/lesson/what-is-psychological-distress-definition-lesson-quiz.html

Sunrise Residential Treatment Center – 4 Steps to Happy Relationships (2018, June 29) Retrieved from https://www.sunrisertc.com/interpersonal-effectiveness/

Sunrise Residential Treatment Center – 6 life changing skills to successfully manage your next emotional crisis (2018, May 21) Retrieved from https://www.sunrisertc.com/distress-tolerance-skills/#tipp

Sunrise Residential Treatment Center – Take Control of Your Emotions Using These 5 Skills (2018, June 29) Retrieved from https://www.sunrisertc.com/dbt-emotion-regulation-skills/

Top 10 Interpersonal Skills: Why They're Important – Interpersonal Skills (n.d.) Retrieved from https://www.wikijob.co.uk/content/interview-advice/competencies/interpersonal-skills

Verywell Mind – Can dialectical behavior therapy help treat your eating disorder? (2019, May 25) retrieved from https://www.verywellmind.com/dialectical-behavior-therapy-for-eating-disorders-1138350

Verywell Mind – How Dialectical Behavior Therapy Improve BPD Distress Tolerance (2019, February 04) Retrieved from https://www.verywellmind.com/distress-tolerance-skills-for-bpd-425372

Verywell Mind – How to Use Mindfulness for PTSD (2019, June 09) retrieved from https://www.verywellmind.com/using-mindfulness-for-ptsd-2797588

Verywell Mind – How to Use Your Innate Distress Tolerance to Manage Intense Emotions (2018, May 07) Retrieved from https://www.verywellmind.com/distress-tolerance-2797294

Verywell Mind – The Benefits of Emotion Regulation Skills for Your Health (2019, May 12) Retrieved from https://www.verywellmind.com/emotion-regulation-skills-training-425374

Verywell Mind – What to Know About Dialectical Behavior Therapy (2019, May 16) Retrieved from https://www.verywellmind.com/dialectical-behavior-therapy-1067402

WebMD – Interpersonal Therapy for Depression (n.d.) Retrieved from https://www.webmd.com/depression/guide/interpersonal-therapy-for-depression#1

Wikipedia – Dialectical Behavior Therapy (2019, June 03) Retrieved from https://en.wikipedia.org/wiki/Dialectical_behavior_therapy

medicine.hsc.wwu.edu - Dialectics in DBT (n.d.) retrieved from https://medicine.hsc.wvu.edu/media/104008/introduction-to-dialectics.pdf

www.ingramcontent.com/pod-product-compliance
Lightning Source LLC
LaVergne TN
LVHW021720060526
838200LV00050B/2772